Leadership Evolution

NAVIGATING CHALLENGES, INSPIRING GROWTH

Leadership Evolution

MURDOCK

PLATYPUS
PUBLISHING

PLATYPUS
PUBLISHING

Platypus Publishing

https://www.rudbits.com/platypus

ISBN: 978-1-965016-00-8

First printing 2024

Copyright © 2024 by Reneé J. Murdock

ACKNOWLEDGMENTS

I dedicate this project to my mother, Mary Etta Carter, who was my biggest cheerleader. She was with me every step of the way until her last breath. I am grateful I was able to experience the love of a mother. She taught me many things through words, actions, and even silence. Thank you, Mom.

Thank you to my husband and daughter who were patient with me. I am grateful you are my family. Love you, infinitely.

Thank you to those who encouraged me along the way. Thank you to the eagle leaders and the duck leaders. Each one of you played a major role in my journey up until now. Nothing was wasted. I am who I am because of the process.

And most of all, thank you to the one on whom my foundation stands, my Abba. You walked with me, carried me, held me, surrounded me, sang over me, strengthened me, and most of all, heard me. You keep me in awe. I love you!

CONTENTS

INTRODUCTION

I have experienced both great and not-so-great leadership. Some leaders have built me up, while others tore me down and trampled on me every chance they got. Sadly, in my first official role as a leader, I was not the one who held others up. I led with fear, shame, hurt, and unforgiveness. I had to learn how to forgive myself and others, admit my mistakes, be settled in my weaknesses, celebrate my strengths, and most importantly, learn to love myself and others. Only then was I able to see how I was not just existing but that *I Was Becoming.*

Getting the most from the book

This is more than just a book; it is a guide to a 56-day journey of discovering the truth about leading yesterday, today, and forevermore. At the end of this journey, you will have a greater understanding of how to live while *becoming* an authentic leader. There is no one like you. No one has your deoxyribonucleic acid (DNA). There is only one blueprint for your makeup. Although there have been and are great leaders in our world, it is not just for a certain type of DNA. The difference between you and them is they learned the art of becoming their authentic selves. To become is to let go of past belief systems of what environments and societal norms have told you about yourself and leadership. Leaders are not born; they are made. The daily and intentional work you are willing to put in will manifest into your becoming.

There are 197 world leaders and 333.34 million companies worldwide. In the United States of America, there are an estimated 11,000 business leaders with the average age being 44 years old. 64.4% are male and 35.6% are female. The top challenge for CEOs is developing the next generation of leaders. The younger generation is leaving organizations for not having the opportunities for self-development and to lead in management roles. Minority groups are not seeing themselves leading in top roles. In the 2023 census report, the top ethnicity group for business leaders is White (67.4%) followed by Hispanic or Latino (15.2%), Asian (6.4%), and Black or African American (6.2%). 83% of business leaders say leadership development is critical, but there are only 5% of businesses that have leadership development programs at all levels. Organizations are having a hard time filling positions when Baby Boomers retire due to the lack of unqualified individuals in soft skills and executive-level skills. Looking at these statistics can help you understand the need for transformational change in our organizations. When you are looking for and desiring change, taking responsibility for your career is key. Use this book as a tool for your leadership toolbox.

Layout of the 56 days

The next 56 days will transform your life inside and out. This book is divided into the top developmental areas of leadership. I encourage you not to read this as a fictional book but to take your time to read each day with the intentionality of meditating, soul searching, and a commitment to act. This will give you time to reevaluate, adjust, and gain a new perspective. Transformation can only take place when you pause and meditate on what you have read. Do not be in a hurry to read through. This is a journey. Think about it as going on a tour with the guide sharing all the wonderful history. When they are done, they give you time to walk around and explore by yourself. This book is a guide, and the time of meditating and reflecting is for you to explore. React and interact with the book. Write, highlight, circle, shout, " uh," "aah," "hmmm " with it. Make it yours.

At the end of each section there are exercises: meditate, observe, and commit.

Meditate: A statement that sums up the daily reading for you to ponder over.

Observation: A reminder to observe your behavior in reference to the topic.

Commit: An action step on the topic of what you will start and stop doing.

There are over 70 impactful statements of influential leaders throughout the book. Go a step further in your journey and research each person and their life to gain a better understanding of how they led.

Seek and Find, Hope and Discover

What we meditate on is what feeds our soul. What feeds our soul feeds the heart. And what is in the heart, we act upon. We, as human beings, are perfectly imperfect. We strive for the top, greatness, and completion. The reality is that all of us are capable of greatness if we choose to be. Striving for the top is striving for the fulfillment of a void. The completion of self is a never-ending journey, for there will always be something missing. We are a repository, a place of storing up, filling up, to hold on to until the items are needed. Once one vessel is filled, we seek for the next one to be filled. We are always realizing something is missing. When that something gets filled, we discover there is something else missing, and then, it gets filled. There is this continual cycle until the day we leave this earth. This is why we are in a state of becoming and not ever finished. If we were ever a finished product, the world would stop growing because we would have stopped growing. No new ideas, discoveries, inventions, or processes will ever come into existence if we become a finished product. Think about the products that exist today. Even they are not finished when discoveries of materials are made. Products are always reforming themselves into what the audience needs before they know they need it.

I hope that every person who decides to take the journey will end in a prosperous place. This journey will be filled with excitement, uncertainty, "aha" moments, newfound passion, and excitement. There might be times when you cry, laugh, regret, accept, admit, and remain silent. It is all a part of the process. I believe we are being re-formalized and remolded while we are relearning and becoming what is needed for the perfect time. I believe in you; now do you believe in yourself?

PART 1

PAINTING THE PORTRAIT OF INTEGRITY

People want power, positions, and benefits, but often do not want the weight of the responsibilities that come with them. Leadership roles are often taken lightly, and the necessary qualifications to get the job done and done right are often not. The character of a person determines their reputation; reputation lasts beyond our lifetime. A moral character must be distinguished from personality.[1] A person can have a strong personality with a weak character. Character is a trait, not an action. It's a state of being. A leader's character is tested every day in every interaction. A leader should be able to answer the following questions:

- Who are you?

- Does your action align with your words?

- What are others saying about you privately and in the open?

These questions reveal the inner workings of a person, and many times, the average person wants to avoid hearing the answers. Whether you are a maintenance worker, cashier, entrepreneur, CEO, or volunteer, who you are would not change based on a function. The jobs just mentioned are functions and not who a person is. How others see us is necessary but not as crucial as our character. Character is who we are when no one is watching. We want a good reputation; having a good name is more than just our reputation. Of course, some may disagree. For too long, we have been taught to keep our reputation intact. We are told not to lie, steal, cheat, and to keep our word, etc. I can do all these things and still lack good character. Are you the type of person who only works hard when those in a higher position are present and then slack off when they leave? Do you only volunteer when senior leaders are in the room? Do you find ways to be seen when "important" people can see or hear you?

My brother once told me that everyone is out for themselves. At first, I was confused and wanted clarity. I asked him to explain because I disagreed with his view. He asked why people

---

1 Richard B. Brandt. (1970). *Traits of Character: A Conceptual Analysis.* American Philosophical Quarterly 1.

get up in the morning and go to work, buy homes, start businesses, and take care of themselves—for themselves, primarily. I still do not agree with his outlook on life; this, of course, is my opinion, and he has the right to his. In those moments, I felt my character was on trial based on the fact that I help others all the time, including him, and I do not do it for myself. I explained to him that when I work, I do it for my family and stay healthy so they do not have to take care of me. When I go to work, yes, I receive a paycheck; my daily goal is to lighten the load of others—we will talk about this later in the book. My volunteering is for someone else. I am not doing it for accolades; I do it because this is who I am. You see, my character means more to me than the world's riches. The reason behind what you do says a lot about your character. The intention of the heart will be displayed in your actions.

There are far too many leaders who lead in immorality. This has been the reason behind many organizations failing, economies falling, and people suffering. Our country has made unethical treaties and is paying the price today. Society tells us the goal is to make it to the top. But what if the goal should be to make it to the bottom? In the Roman era, there were amphitheaters, where the seats were arranged in a circular setting, tiered going up with the center at the bottom. The word "amphitheater" in Greek means "on both sides" or "around" for viewing. To be viewed was to be at the center in an open space where everyone could see from all sides and different angles. In today's society, we do not invite others to view us openly from all sides. We would rather hide in the rafters but still want to be seen and heard. To be heard is to be seen, and to be seen is an invitation to be examined. Leading is an examination of word and deed at any given moment. The people in those audiences had a right to have an opinion based on their experience based on what they saw and heard. When theaters shifted to raised platforms with the seating below, the mindset of how we view leading and others completely changed. Leading became about ownership, rulership, and dominating over others. Now, we are spending time and money to help shift how we think about ourselves and others.

Character is the foundation of leadership: integrity, humility, accountability, and courage.[2]

Foundation of Character	
Integrity	Accept awards when they do the work and are not ashamed to say who they are and what they believe.
Humility	Keep the ego intact, rejoice with others on their successes, and make individuals willing to change.
Accountability	Willing to answer for results, do not mind being measured, and finish what they start.
Courage	Resist and challenge the status quo. Create—not just take care of. There is an emotional, intellectual, spiritual, and physical burden to bear. Maintain discipline to make it happen.

People who examine themselves daily can answer the question of why they do what they do. Of course, the stage is not the goal; however, you know that with exemplary character, whether you are on the stage or not, there is no hiding who you are, and others can view you and will form their own opinion. Your behavior starts from the posture of your heart; everything else flows from it.

Let us take the next seven days to journey on developing moral character. You may say that your character is intact, and this section does not apply to you. This book is for growth and development as a leader. No one has arrived and no longer needs improvement. Even John Maxwell has found himself, as he gets older, spending less time talking and more time observing and applying. Take each day to meditate on the readings, observe behaviors, commit to change, and start to apply those commitments. Growing as a leader takes work. As you go through this section, remember that your character speaks when you are present and when you are gone.

2 Clark, T. R. (2016). *Leading with character and competence : moving beyond title, position, and authority.* Berrett-Koehler Publishers.

DAY 1

"If you don't have an ethical creed that goes to your marrow and says, 'some things are not for sale at any price,' you are for sale. You will go to the highest bidder."
— **Timothy Clark**

Society teaches that integrity is no longer of extended importance and is unrealistic. If you are going to win, you have to do it at all costs: lie, steal, cheat, extort, bribe, and bend the rules to get what you want. We can all agree that the world is corrupt and courage is hard to come by regarding ethical behavior. You don't even have to hunt down situations to improve in this area. The situations will find you and test you until you either overcome the corruption or give in. You can even convince your conscience to let you believe you made the right decision.

"Are you for sale?" Timothy Clark poses this question to leaders during his sessions. Some individuals will say, "No, I cannot be bought." But can you? Have you? When it comes to contracts and hiring, there is often a conflict of interest when you know the individuals and are in a position to determine who gets in and who does not. Have you ever placed job announcements and written them specifically for someone to ensure they get hired? Have you ever altered the time you worked telling yourself they owe you? Have you ever taken supplies from the office for personal use? Have you ever lied to employees to cover the tracks of leaders' mistakes? Have you ever used your position or title to get what you want? Have you ever been on Facebook, Twitter, Instagram, or other social media platforms during work hours? All of these questions address the top unethical behaviors that occur in the workplace. Transgressions do not start off big; they begin small and grow until someone finds themselves down a mudslide.

There is a show that is in the top 10 on Netflix called "Suits." This show was introduced to me by my husband, and it became the only show we could watch together. I joined in on season 3 and had to catch up on who was who and the firm's layout. The show is based on Mike Ross (Adams), who uses his photographic memory to land a job as an associate with big-shot lawyer Harvey Spector (Gabriel Macht). Harvey takes Mike on as an associate at his firm, even though Mike has never been to law school but has passed the LSAT multiple times by taking it as a proxy for others. Every episode encompasses attempting to keep Mike's secret. The partners eventually find out but keep him on because they are winning cases; simply put, he is making them money. If you have not seen the show, you probably ask the same question: Why didn't he go to law school? Well, he got accepted but was blackballed because he took the LSAT for the Dean's daughter, and she got caught. In each episode, I would ask, "Why don't they send him to school? He has contacts now, and I am sure the blackball will be lifted." I would say this same thing each time, and my husband would give me this side glance (we have heard they are not sending him). The world I live in says, "Let us make it right: you can work here. We will pay for your school, as long as you agree to stay on after graduating for X number of years. In my world, things are simple and recompensable.

The reason why this is important is because each day, you will be faced with the decision of whether you are for sale and at what price. There would not have been nine seasons if they had sent Mike back to school. When we place the welfare of ourselves above others, we have put a price on our character. I can guarantee that unethical behavior will or is around you each day. The goal is to be prepared for how to handle such situations. The situation will not come gift-wrapped with a note, "Hi, I am in an unethical situation." Preparation is knowing who you are and what you stand for. MBA graduates are taking a Volunteer Oath to remind them of their responsibilities. The oath starts with:

As a business leader, I recognize my role in society.

My purpose is to lead people and manage resources to create value that no single individual can create alone.

My decisions affect the well-being of individuals inside and outside my enterprise, today and tomorrow.

It goes on to state seven things they promise to do. Leaders who lack moral character must be governed by laws, rules, policies, etc. But even then, these are meant to be broken. Morality is not learned through reading; it is by acting or not acting. Outside those governing policies, you should have your creed, principles, and Magna Carta to stand on. Will you be a leader who will stand up for what is right or be bogged with the pressures of the culture and norms?

Exercise

Meditate: What is the price for becoming a leader?

Observe: What unethical behavior have I witnessed or partaken in?

Commit: Develop a personal ethics creed on what I promise to uphold daily.

DAY 2

"Healing restores the soul."
— **Unknown**

When we think of a leader's character, most would not equate healing as one of those traits. I have yet to come across any corporate organization that trains on healing. Even in religious organizations, it is not a requirement to heal first before volunteering or being appointed as a leader. You have heard the saying before: hurt people, hurt people. When people are not healed, they will project those disappointments, rejections, hurts, and pains onto others, ultimately walking in unforgiveness. If we had more training on how to forgive our workforce, it would look completely different. Can you imagine coming to work or other work efforts when people know how to forgive? People would be laughing, smiling, asking about each other's day, listening to one another, being mindful of others, and making everyone feel included. They wouldn't be easily offended and would ask questions instead of attacking or retreating. This is achievable, but only if we start with ourselves.

I remember when I would put on a happy face, but inside I was upset when I was not asked to join to be a part of something. I was doing an excellent job of hiding, but eventually, what was on the inside was displayed on the outside. I was always on the defensive, ready to attack at any given moment. I had issues of rejection, and this affected every area of my life. My expectations of myself were unrealistic, and I placed those exact expectations on others. Once I identified the root cause of rejection, abandonment, and humiliation, I was able to start the healing process of forgiveness, starting with myself. From a young age, I always felt different and abandoned. I do not know the name of the man who helped conceive me or his family. This left me with a sense of not being wanted. According to psychologist Lisa Bourbeau, problems stem from five wounds to the soul: rejection, abandonment, humiliation, betrayal, and injustice.[3] In each of these wounds, there are specific masks we wear.[4]

Once I was able to deal with the reality that I may never know who my father is or his family, I realized that those facts do not predict my value as a human being. Forgiving myself of the shame, hurt, and pain associated with rejection allowed me to forgive others quickly. My beautiful smile was no longer fake; it was the joy from the inside displaying on the outside. People would ask me why I was smiling so hard, why I was so happy, and why I smiled all the time. I was able to answer these questions honestly. The joy I have found is not based on my past, present, or future. The knowing of who you are and whom you belong to was my position of peace. This is not to say disappointment or disagreements never happen. The difference now is that my response comes from a healthy place and not from a place of hurt.

Emotional and mental healing are just as important as physical healing. The mind, will, and emotions make up our soul. Each of these components is essential in ensuring they are healthy. Leaders need sound thinking when leading. Where do knowledge, insight, and revelation happen in the mind? As a leader I need to know what to seek in making decisions that are good for all and not just me, myself, and I. How we love, grieve, and show grace and mercy comes from our emotions. Leaders must be willing to show their emotions to free others to do the same. Leading from a healthy place allows others to see the

3 Bourbeau. L. (2020). Heal your wounds & find your true self: Finally, a book that explains why it's so hard being yourself! Editions E.T.C. Inc.
4 Audi, Robert. (1997). *Moral Knowledge and Ethical Character.* Oxford University Press, Incorporated. ProQuest Ebook Central. http://ebookcentral.proquest.com/lib/regent-ebooks/detail.action?docID=272329.

person for who they truly are and not a made-up version based on circumstances. There are things in life that have beaten up our souls, and we go through life living incomplete or believing everyone is against us when, in fact, we have just believed the lies. Restoring our soul is finding true joy, healing, and peace. Followers want to follow those who are genuinely concerned about their welfare. Can you truly be concerned and help others grow if you are living in unforgiveness?

Exercise

Meditate: Healing starts by forgiving myself first.

Observe: Am I in an unhealthy place in my soul? What is the root cause of my pain?

Commit: Develop a list of areas where I must forgive myself and others. Look in the mirror and tell myself I am forgiven. Forgive others who have done me wrong. Practice forgiveness every day.

DAY 3

"He has honor if he holds himself to an ideal of conduct though it is inconvenient, unprofitable, or dangerous to do so."
— **Walter Lippmann**

We all know the right things to do, but we do not always choose to do the right things. We would rather take the path that seems to be an easy shortcut. Leadership is honorable, not because of power but because of the servitude toward others. Changing the life of one person affects the lives of others. Your character will influence others to either follow or divert. Individuals can be on your team, but that does not necessarily mean they are following you. Doing what is right can be inconvenient and is often frowned upon. There is pressure from culture, society, peers, time, and expectations. The question is, will you give in to those pressures?

Going against what is considered "normal" takes courage and can sometimes be dangerous. There is always the risk of being an outcast for standing up for the truth. I would rather be in the lion's den than have my character derailed. The daily conversations we have can derail our character—those conversations we like to label as "venting" when, in fact, they involve mishandling others' character. I often wonder why leaders speak negatively about their superiors instead of having hard conversations. Once you have the conversation about their behavior or situation, leave it there in the room. When we take the conversation from its proper place, it causes plagues to break out among the people. Lippmann was a revolutionary figure in journalism during his era. He challenged the writers and audience on how they viewed the facts. Lippmann argued that people believe the pictures in their heads rather than engaging in critical thinking. Because of this, there has been an ineffective way to bring information to the media.[5] Are we not still dealing with this issue today—painting pictures for the audience rather than presenting facts? I am sure he was not the favorite of many politicians and others in positions of social holdings. Lippmann quit his job as secretary to George R. Lunn after four months because Lunn did not fulfill his duties as stated on socialism. Are you willing to walk away from what seems prestigious to uphold your morals and values?

No one wakes up and says, "I will break the rules today." The pressures around them cause individuals to give in to those shortcuts. If a person has not been tested and tried to develop their character, they cannot stand up for what they know to be correct. I have stayed in places where my values did not align with theirs. I realized that by staying, I agreed with what they were doing. I made a decision: my values were far more critical than a connection, network, or community could ever offer or provide my peace, so I left. I told myself I would never compromise my truths in the name of "religious power beliefs." Eric Zorn, a Chicago Tribune columnist, says a person of character has a conscience (Gini & Green, 2013). They are aware of, sensitive to, and can make sound judgments about interactions with others.

As you take the time to develop your character, remember that courage is warranted. Even though you may be left without, the empty place of community will afford you opportunities to connect with those who are courageous enough to do the right things in times of opposition.

Exercise

Meditate: True honor is holding to what is honest and right.

Observe: Are there areas where I have compromised what is right?

Commit: Take the steps to speak out on mistruths. Hold myself and others accountable for what was promised.

---

5 Lippmann, W. & Merz, C. (1920). *A Test of the News.*

DAY 4

"Our life is what our thoughts make it"
— **Marcus Aurelius**

Developing your character is about being accountable for how you think. The thoughts result in behavior. If you think about negative things all the time, then you are believing in those things. The phrase "I cannot" is not allowed in my household. If you say you cannot, then yes, you cannot. It is okay to say, "This is challenging; I will do my best." By saying so, I have acknowledged that this does not come naturally, and I am willing to give it all I have. Leading is looking at challenges as opportunities, not as limitations.

We have all encountered situations where there is a person in the group who is a downer; no matter what is said or done, their negativity spills all over the place. You may find yourself annoyed, frustrated, or caving into this type of thinking: "Man, they are right; this will never work. There needs to be more time; it did not work before, so why keep trying?" I was in a meeting, and a person was going on and on about how hard it would be to bring someone on. They said, "It will take too long; we need them to be able to do the work now." I chimed in, speaking to the group about how we are all capable human beings and if taught correctly, they would get up to speed. I explained what work they could do right out of the gate and how we should give them the work that required more skills, train them, and be there through the process until it was time to release the handlebars. I said this for the group to see what was possible because this individual had a defeatist attitude. My job was to present optimism. The group shifted from defeat to "we can make it happen."

Leaders whose character is developed do not allow the weight of the world to hold them back from winning. Every influential person has said the same thing:

- I jumped without a parachute.

- I did not allow the "no" to stop me from what I believed in.

- The opinions of others were just that—their opinions.

- If no one else believed, I had to.

Those thoughts are what got them to where they are today. You ought to think about things that are lovely and true. What are the things that are lovely? Maybe it's the air you breathe, your health, a sound mind, your family, a job, the green grass, the blowing leaves, the watering rain, and much more. You have to open up your eyes to see all the lovely things that surround you. Those true things are culture, society, job, family, and health. There are others; the point is that the truth, at times, is unpleasant, but it is also equally pleasing. Now, if you have yet to take a course or have been trained to fly an airplane, the truth is that you would not be able to fly at the moment. However, can you get there? Yes. How you think is how you see the world; how you see the world is how you will lead. Martin Luther King Jr. saw the world as equal, and Adolf Hitler saw liberal Judaism, Marxism, and secularism as the enemy. Two different views, two different causes, and two different outcomes. In both, there were unpleasantries, but there was also beauty.

Developing positive thinking can only be done with mental rehearsal[6] and humor. Do not take yourself too seriously; laugh often at the things you do. Former President Ronald Reagan said to doctors when wounded from an assassination attempt, "Please tell me you are Republicans." His humor and positive thinking brought ease to family, friends, staff, and the country.

---

6 Hackman, M. Z., & Johnson, C. E. (2013). Leadership: A communication perspective (Sixth ed.). Waveland Press.

Leading with the right thinking can change how others view themselves and the world. There is no reason why you cannot become an effective leader if you set goals and stick to them.

Exercise

Meditate: What is lovely and what is true?

Observe: How many times am I saying "*I cannot*"?

Commit: Take the "I cannot" and change them to "I can" and "I will." Be honest and realistic.

DAY 5

"It is not what the person may feel about himself as to his honesty, but how others read him"
— Ted W. Engstrom

Would you follow someone who has not put themselves out there as honest and dependable? If it does not cost you, no one is buying it. Followers want to trust in their leader and know that when it gets tough, they are willing to put themselves out there. When they do, followers will do so in return. You may think you are putting yourself out there, but we should not think too highly of ourselves and allow the ego to take over. One way to give your ego an eviction notice is to cultivate your character.

We talked about power the other day. Power is not given; it is earned by putting in the work. Do you want power? Get authority. Do you want authority? Cultivate your character. To say if you had more authority, you would get more done is a sad excuse because you can do something about it. [7]Competency, position, personality, and character are areas you have the power to change. Is it easy for people to talk to you and share information, both personal and professional, or do you feel like you are always in the dark? The easier it is for followers to share, talk, and listen, the easier work becomes. I heard this from another leader: if an employee feels like they have to do extra work in figuring out how to approach their supervisor, it's like having another inherent job. When given too much work, something tends to slip through the cracks. Leaders should not place unnecessary work on others.

7 Engstrom, T. (1978). The making of a Christian leader: How to develop management and human relations skills. Zondervan.

As we go through life, we create trails. Think about what type of trails you have created and who would follow them. Are there explosive devices along the path, weeds that have overgrown, or muddy areas with wormholes? Or has the path been cleared for others to walk through while feeling safe, secure, and confident they are going in the right direction? The character of a person speaks loudly and provides clear guidance on who they are. A conversation arose about one of my previous leaders, and I disagreed with what was being said because it was not my experience. I let the person know that was not my experience and that they were a good leader. I could have sat and gone along to get in touch with the person. I decided to stand for my truth in the matter. Now, the person knows how I feel about the matter and that I am willing to put myself out there for others.

Leadership is about others and how they are served, treated, guided, valued, and developed. Serving others takes character development and understanding the actual cause. There should be a "leadership awareness ribbon" so individuals are more mindful of the responsibilities of leading. Peter Drucker insists that leadership is about growing and developing the collective human experience.[8] Charisma will only carry a person so far; moral character will carry a lifetime. A leader is virtuous. There is substance, a natural substance; the dramatics are not necessary because there are values and integrity.[9]

You may think you are the best thing since Chick-fil-A sauce, but what do others know to be true about your integrity? It should allow others to sing praises and not be about you providing the tune. People will follow and do more when they believe and trust in their leaders. It is hard to say no to someone who you know has your best interests at heart.

---

8 Drucker, P. F. (January 1988). *"Leadership: more doing than dash."* The Wall Street Journal. Gini, A., & Green, R. M. (2013). *10 virtues of outstanding leaders leadership & character.* John Wiley & Sons Inc.

9 Sosik, J. J. (2015). *Leading with character: stories of valor and virtue and the principles they teach (Second edition.).* Information Age Publishing, Inc.

Exercise

Meditate: Leadership is not about being given authority; it has to be earned by putting myself out there.

Observe: Do I fail to be honest with myself and others? Am I tooting my own horn? What do others say about my honesty?

Commit: Find out what motivates your team members and/or peers.

DAY 6

"Wealth is physical, while character is spiritual."
— **Reneé Murdock**

There are two questions we all have asked ourselves at least once: Why am I here, and how did I get here? Depending on your journey in faith, you have probably already discovered the answers to these questions. I am not here to force my faith—I will share my views on finding the answer for myself. We have these two questions because God depended on humanity to search for something greater than themselves. In the search, you will discover Him and who you are. This can only be done through internal work. I was walking through the neighborhood with my husband and my daughter's dog, and I started having flashbacks from when we first moved in. Now, I am not a country girl; I did marry a country boy who likes land and things. As such, I remember asking him numerous times to get on the grass. I wanted it to look nice and green like our previous residence (a different state). I am sure he was tired of me saying something; he would say it would take time. He had placed fertilizer, cow manure and put down topsoil in certain areas and it still was not a lush green. After a while, I asked him about one neighbor whose grass was beautiful year-round. Is it real? Come to find out it's because the neighbor installed an underground fertilizing system while the house was getting built. All he did was put the fertilizers in a tank system, and it dispense when the grass is watered. Here is what I learned from my walk that day; You will only get the results you want if you go deep and put in the work. Character development is going to take time.

Benjamin Franklin would write down how he fared with the 13 virtues he lived by. What are yours? As he went on through life, there were days he did well, and days he did not. He gave up his internal work for he felt mastering them would have him lose humility. While I disagree with Mr. Franklin, no creature is perfect. He had the right concept in taking inventory of progress by observing and writing it down. Developing good character does not mean you will lack humility; you will have humility resolved. Mr. Franklin did not want to dig those trenches or go out to treat the yard to keep the grass healthy and beautiful.

On the other hand, many have continued the journey of character development and have been able to influence millions. By doing so, they, in turn, have helped develop others. Is it not the ultimate goal of leadership to multiply other great leaders? We have to stop looking at the outward, tangible things, and seek those things that cannot be seen.

Taking the steps of doing a daily devotion of meditation and reflection is a great starting point. As you go through this journey, your past will come back to haunt you and put you to shame. You must overcome those evil thoughts for you are not defined by your past if you don't allow it. Look toward the future, see the good end, and keep your eyes focused there. Some have had the opportunity, like my neighbor, to start from the beginning before leaving home or taking on a leadership role. Others are like my yard where things were placed on top, and they may not realize how much the cost will eventually be. Now, I humbly submit to my husband these thoughts when planning projects: let us do it now and do it right, because eventually, it has to be done. When it comes back around, the cost will be higher. Sosik says character development starts as a child in how we are raised. [10] If we are taught to be good to others, honest, kind, and fair, these foundational principles are built on by other community factors. Youth are impressionable and will take in what they hear, see, and experience. This is why de-

10 Sosik, J. J. (2015). Leading with character: stories of valor and virtue and the principles they teach (Second edition.). Information Age Publishing, Inc.

veloping character is essential for all who play a part in society, whether you are a business owner, teacher, banker, police officer, firefighter, veteran, principal, custodian, engineer, graphic designer, chief, clergy, doctor, lawyer, scientist, or artist. In each of these fields, we touch others and impact the world we live in. Spiritual health brings physical wealth.

Exercise

Meditate: Not to conform to my past, but to look to the future.

Observe: What things did I do well and stay true to my virtues? What things could have been done better?

Commit: Regarding the things that I did not do well, write down how I will approach them next time and do as such. What went well? Keep doing and observing.

DAY 7

Take time today to review the past six days and write down five virtues you will stay true to, or go over the ones you already have and adjust as needed.

- Why did you choose these virtues?

- Have those virtues been compromised this week?

- What areas have you done well in? What areas did you struggle with?

- What have others said about you this week that you agree or disagree with?

In the coming week, find three leaders and ask them what their virtues are and what they do daily to stay true to them.

The foundation of leadership is character. Your character says who you are when you are not speaking and when you are not in the room. It speaks loudly and strongly, whether it is good or bad. People will want to duplicate or disregard your intentions. The character of a person tells others how they feel about you. If people do not value themselves, they definitely will not value others. The goal of leadership is to influence others to become who they indeed are; this is only possible if you are your true self. The excuse of "this is me" is not acceptable. The development of character is groundbreaking work. There are no fancy machines or shortcuts. There is, however, wisdom and insight of those who have taken the journey. We look at their lives and reflect on the honesty of disabling strengths and weaknesses.

We are not perfect, and perfection is not the end goal. Can people trust you with their hearts, families, money, property, dreams, and visions? Will you live a life of being honest with yourself first and with others? Only time will tell. Transformation is not easy, nor is it a quick fix. The transformational leader is living a life of authenticity and a transformed mindset. They are putting aside the old ways of living because they did not work and are deciding to become their true selves and share themselves with the world to free others. Remember, the season changes, and fertilization will always be necessary to keep the grass flourishing.

References

Audi, R. (1997). *Moral knowledge and ethical character*. Oxford University Press. http://ebookcentral.proquest.com/lib/regent-ebooks/detail.action?docID=272329

Bourbeau, L. (2020). *Heal your wounds & find your true self: Finally, a book that explains why it's so hard being yourself!*. Editions E.T.C. Inc.

Clark, T. R. (2016). *Leading with character and competence: Moving beyond title, position, and authority*. Berrett-Koehler Publishers.

Drucker, P. F. (1988, January 6). Leadership: More doing than dash. *The Wall Street Journal*.

Engstrom, T. (1978). *The making of a Christian leader: How to develop management and human relations skills*. Zondervan.

Gini, A., & Green, R. M. (2013). *10 virtues of outstanding leaders: Leadership & character*. John Wiley & Sons.

Hackman, M. Z., & Johnson, C. E. (2013). *Leadership: A communication perspective* (6th ed.). Waveland Press.

Leggett, B. (2012, June 29). Profile of a great persuader: Ronald Reagan - Rhetoric and leadership: Soft power. *Rhetoric and Leadership: Soft Power - Brian O'C Leggett's Blog*. https://blog.iese.edu/leggett/2012/06/29/profile-of-a-great-persuader-ronald-reagan/

Lippmann, W., & Merz, C. (1920). A test of the news.

Brandt, R. B. (1970). Traits of character: A conceptual analysis. *American Philosophical Quarterly, 1*.

Thomas, L. (1989). *Living morally: A psychology of moral character*. Temple University Press.

Sosik, J. J. (2015). *Leading with character: Stories of valor and virtue and the principles they teach* (2nd ed.). Information Age Publishing.

PART 2

MIRROR, MIRROR

The advancement of technology is growing each day and has caused social interactions to become less and less. There are disconnects in homes and workplaces. Humans interact with machines more than with one another. If given a choice between meeting in person or virtually, the majority will choose virtual. Individuals will spend more time on gadgets than on having a meal together. Do not get me wrong; I will be the first to raise my hand in favor of technological advancement. But I am for both technology *and* social interactions. Technology is a beautiful and dreadful creation all in one. Previous generations have the experience of building meaningful relationships while the current generations have friends through a gaming system. I cannot tell you how many times I have heard or had personal knowledge of friend groups or dating from an online connection. Marriage, divorce, and serious crimes have taken place in this make-believe world of true intimacy. A survey showed people spend, on average, 8 hours a day on a screen, and 2 hours of that time is spent on social media. Teenagers, between ages 15 and 18, spend the most time on screens compared to any other group.[11] What is this saying? People are losing touch with their emotional intelligence and would rather isolate themselves from others. There are concerns that Artificial Intelligence (AI) will take jobs away. Can AI connect, feel, touch, or comfort? No. AI will bring jobs because it cannot replace human connection. The social link among humans lets me know there will always be a job for leaders.

Emotional Intelligence (EI) comprises five components: self-awareness, self-regulation, self-motivation, social skills, and empathy. The EI model is broken down into two major parts: managing oneself and managing others. A person will be unable to influence others without being able to manage themselves. Self-awareness is being aware of our psychological state at any time. There is a deep understanding of thoughts, feelings, behavior, strengths, weaknesses, drives, and needs.

---

11 Rothwell, J. (2024, February 9). *Teens spend average of 4.8 hours on social media per day.* Gallup.com. https://news.gallup.com/poll/512576/teens-spend-average-hours-social-media-per-day.aspx

LEADERSHIP EVOLUTION

¹² There is a sensitivity to what is happening around you. When we are unaware of ourselves, we tend to do and say things that harm others. We are frivolous with our words. Let me talk about myself. I would walk around and say things and keep it moving. I was completely unaware of how I came across, made others feel, or even how I felt about those encounters. I was utterly incognizant of my behavior. When someone, such as family, friends, co-workers, or a boss, makes us angry, it affects our pride, self-esteem, and security. Having self-awareness is being honest and realistic.

Influential leaders have high EI. This is not to say leaders with high EI do not make mistakes. They are aware of their conduct and others' feelings around them. Self-awareness is essential when it comes to leadership growth. The reality is that many more people do not know themselves than the ones who do. People tend to go through the motions of life on autopilot. Why do you think there are hundreds of books on "finding yourself" or "how to love yourself" and testimonies on discovering yourself? Take a moment to answer the following questions:

What is your favorite…

Actor/actress Architectural style of buildings Artist Movie App	Book Candle scent Clothing material Cologne/Perfume Color	Flower Food Fruit Game Hairstyle	Music era Purse/bag style School subject Sitcom Soap	Soup Sport Store Technology brand Vegetable

What makes you…

Angry Anxious	Cry Dance	Disappointed Laugh	Shout Smile Stand Still

---

12 Purushothaman, R. (2021). *Emotional intelligence.* SAGE Publications India Pvt, Ltd.

This might be hard to answer. If you had asked me these questions years ago, I would not have had an answer to each one. However, now I do. It was easier for me to say what I did not like. Can you imagine the pain I put my husband through? I would often wonder why he did not know what I liked. Well, I didn't know either.

Let us take the next seven days to journey through growing in self-awareness. Take each day to meditate on the readings, observe behaviors, commit to change, and start to apply those commitments. Growing as a leader takes work. Remember, as you go through this section, leaders are not afraid to express their emotions and handle others with care.

DAY 1

"The best and most beautiful things in the world cannot be seen or even touched. They must be felt with the heart."
— Helen Keller

Emotions are a natural, instinctive state of mind that derives from one's circumstances, mood, or relationships with others. We all feel things. Sometimes those things are good, bad, or indifferent, but the feelings are always there. You do not need physical sight to see or feel. There are things we may miss if we are only looking with our physical senses. There is a taboo that we are not to express our feelings, especially outside the comfort of our homes. Anne Sullivan empathized with Helen Keller. Anne knew Helen desired to communicate and experience the world like those around her.[13] If not, she would not lash out; her actions were saying, "I am here, I am alive, I want to be part of the world, but I do not know how."

Expressing oneself is not a weakness; it says you are alive. Whatever the expression is, you now know how you feel about a particular situation. This is not a rite of passage to haul off on individuals in meetings. I do not believe Anne realized it at the time, but she had a high level of Emotional Intelligence. EI is a relationship between emotions, feelings, and behavior.[14] I once encountered an individual, and the situation could have gone better if I had more EI at the time. Emotions were high, and nothing, I mean nothing, was accomplished. That evening,

---

13 Nielsen, K. E. (2009). *Beyond the Miracle Worker: The remarkable life of Anne Sullivan Macy and her extraordinary friendship with Helen Keller.* Beacon Press.

14 Norris, C. J., Chen, E. E., Zhu, D. C., Small, S. L., & Cacioppo, J. T. (2004). *The Interaction of Social and Emotional Processes in the Brain. Journal of Cognitive Neuroscience*, 16(10), 1818–1829. https://doi.org/10.1162/0898929042947847

I felt terrible and did some self-reflection on what I could have done differently and why I had become angry in the first place. I returned the next day, apologized for my behavior, and shared what bothered me rather than attacking someone for what they did.

People with a high level of self-awareness can recognize their feelings and those of the people around them.[15] I missed the mark that day on being self-aware because I allowed the behavior to be the critical factor in how I responded. As leaders, there will be times when a team member will make mistakes. The goal is not to address the behavior itself, but rather their emotions. There is always an underlying reasoning, and the question is, will you listen to the behavior or the heart? Do not walk by people when you see them reaching out for help; instead, stop and offer a hand.

Exercise

Meditate: Think about beautiful things that cannot be seen or touched.

Observe: What things have I walked past without giving consideration?

Commit: Every day, I will listen with my heart and not my ears when others speak.

---

15 Norris, C. J., Chen, E. E., Zhu, D. C., Small, S. L., & Cacioppo, J. T. (2004). *The Interaction of Social and Emotional Processes in the Brain. Journal of Cognitive Neuroscience*, 16(10), 1818–1829. https://doi.org/10.1162/0898929042947847

DAY 2

"You have to get people to experience what you are explaining;
understanding will come in a deeper way."
— Kouzes & Posner

We often encounter and read about leaders who have inspired the world. We use them as measuring sticks for our capabilities to have the same effect on others. They had a cause: hunger, racial injustice, war crimes, depression, recession, or terrorism. You say to yourself that there is no such cause here, just merely everyday work. There is a natural human tendency to compare ourselves to others. Comparing yourself is an insult. You are correct; you will never be Martin Luther King Jr. or Mother Teresa. Why? Because there was and will be only one of those leaders. Just like there is only one of you. Comparing your capabilities with others will not allow you to become the leader you are meant to be.

The only difference between you and those inspiring leaders is that they understood how to use their emotions to get people to listen, understand, and act. Think about how they got you to donate to a charity, volunteer, or vote for a particular effort. I will tell you how—the person used emotions to draw their audience into the story. We tend to shy away from our emotions and believe it is a hindrance rather than an advantage. Mother Teresa used her passion to get people to act. What do you believe in? What are you passionate about? Use that drive to lead. It is essential to know why you are working and how the work ties into your belief system.

I have volunteered on many projects, and getting volunteers to commit over a long period of time is challenging. The key to keeping a volunteer team together over time is tapping into their emotions. I usually remind them of why they joined and the difference they have made since joining, and with their help, we could achieve even more. I use a life story they can relate to. In meetings, I share photos of those we helped and use quotes from leaders and those we served. I use symbolic language to tap into their emotions.

Again, emotions are not destructive, nor are they a weakness. Emotions make things more memorable. Think about watching a short video on Instagram versus reading the story. In the video, you can see, hear, and feel the person's emotions about the subject. James McGaugh, a professor of neurobiology, points out, "Whether implicit or explicit, our memories connect the past to the present and allow us to form expectations of the future. They are our most important assets, and without them, life as we know it would be impossible.[16] If you are wondering why the team is not responding, try expressing your emotions next time. Telling someone to do something will not get them to respond; tapping into their emotions will. Change starts with how a person feels.

Exercise

Meditate: Comparing myself to others is not wise; it will only lead to envy and jealousy.

Observe: Who am I comparing myself to and why?

Commit: Stop comparing and start celebrating my strengths. In the subsequent meetings/encounters with the person I compare myself to, celebrate them instead. Write down or voice record a story based on a topic the initiative needs to get done and share it with the team.

---

16 McGaugh, J. L. (2003). *Memory and emotion: The making of lasting memories*. Columbia University Press.

DAY 3

"Look outside and you will see yourself. Look inside and you will find yourself."
— **Drew Gerald**

There is an old saying that goes, "If you point one finger, there are three more pointing back at you." I am not sure how many times you heard this growing up or maybe you have adopted it yourself. This simple saying reminds us not to focus on others but to look at ourselves first. Self-reflection is challenging when you do not want to be the cause of error. There is no getting past mistakes. Everyone makes them no matter how much one tries to prevent them.

When I was a child, people would call me ugly, black, skinny, scrawny, and with big teeth. They would laugh at my clothes, shoes, and my hair. Of course, I had self-image issues. I went through the majority of my life believing those words. I used to cover my smile with my hands and could not stand to look in the mirror. What I saw, I did not like. I used other things to make me feel good about myself: clothes, hair, and shoes. They gave me my identity. This only worked for so long; I noticed that how I felt on the inside determined how I reflected on the outside. My attitude could have been better. I had a rough exterior to portray that nothing could get to me, harm me, or move me. In fact, I automatically went on the defensive. I was a master at it. But doing so caused more problems in the way I was leading myself and others. A person once told me, "I do not like this person, but I like this person." They were referring to me—there were two sides. I ate those words, and I had to digest them. In conclusion, I wanted to be the same person regardless of where I was.

When we are unaware that destruction is not that far behind, we suffer, our teams suffer, and organizations suffer. Self-awareness is not only about knowing about yourself; it is also about being present. What is happening right now—not yesterday or in the future? You are mindful of the moment, you are engaged, and you understand how you are feeling and how others are feeling. You may be anxious, tired, or upset, and that's okay. Awareness allows you to be in control rather than lose it. If you are genuinely aware of how you are responding emotionally, you are in a better position to bring about clarity.[17]

The only way to find yourself is to look inward. I had to learn to do internal work to get to the root causes of my anger, hurt, disappointment, and unforgiveness. I needed a new heart, a plausible heart, a heart that was softened. What goes on in the heart is poured out. Forgiveness was the key to unlocking all the other stuff that was going on in my heart. The more I forgave, the quicker I forgave, and the more sensitive I was about the things happening around me. I was understanding how my emotions worked and was able to be in control of my behavior. I was happy; my smile was genuine. What was happening on the inside was showing on the outside. Leaders who are aware are transformational. They put in the work each day to renew their mind and guard their heart. They willfully humble themselves.

Exercise

Meditate: Look within to find the true me.

Observe: What happens when I get upset or disagree? How does my body respond? How do others respond?

Commit: Laying my ego down daily and picking up the heart of the matter. Turn off notifications on computers, put the phone on silent, put the device down, and take the time to be present today, tomorrow, and every time I am with others.

---

17 Gonzalez, M. (2012). *Mindful Leadership the 9 ways to self-awareness, transforming yourself, and inspiring others (1st edition)*. Jossey-Bass.

DAY 4

"There is a deeper engagement of the shadow side of self - the parts of us we have ignored and not developed."
-Anderson & Adams

A shadow is not this over-looming thing in our lives; there is a blind spot we are unaware of. Because we are unaware, it has been ignored, forgotten about, and is underdeveloped. Let's talk about the natural physics of the human body. We all have a muscular system. The system is what makes us move in response to our brains. In his book, "The Human Body Atlas: How the Human Body Works," Professor Ken Ashwell breaks down the muscular system and explains how it encompasses the skeletal muscles of the body, which are voluntary muscles. Underneath the skin's surface are the skeletal muscles that cover the body and make up our physique. There are 700 muscles in the human body and they make up 60 percent of the body's total weight. These muscles are arranged in layers; superficial ones lie close to the surface while deep ones are closer to the organs to protect them. The muscles need oxygen and glucose for movement.[18] Okay, you did not come for an anatomy class, but we can see how our bodies are made in layers and how each layer provides some significance. The deeper the layer, the more critical the work. This is why we cannot go to the gym for two weeks and think a six-pack will be on display. Many people have quit before they even started; the pain, soreness, and change of pace become too much. What happens is those muscles go back to being underdeveloped, and when deciding to return to the gym, the process starts all over again.

18 Ashwell, K. (2016). *The human body atlas: How the human body works.* Quarto Publishing.

Ignoring something does not mean it does not exist. There was a conscious decision not to give attention to a matter. You hope for change but want to stay the same. You hope for different results but do the same things. You think about what needs to be done, but those thoughts remain thoughts. Leading in a world that will change without our permission means we need to be ready and willing to be a part of making those changes. There is inner work that has to be done daily to develop self-awareness. Watch your emotions and how you respond to situations and conversations. I used to become annoyed when people would start a meeting late to the point that I could not concentrate because the meeting started late. The meeting would be ongoing, and I would be preoccupied with why they were late. It took me a while to realize that everyone does not value what I value, and I should not judge them based on their different values. After talking to the individual, I learned they did not view the meeting as starting late. They wanted to take time for people to relax so the meeting could be productive. We can only know what we know if we ask. There is a tendency to blame external factors when emotions show up. We have been taught to suppress them: "Stop crying," "That did not hurt," "There is no point," "There is no reason to be upset," and "We do not allow people to see us sweat." Adults have passed this down from generation to generation. They mean well but cause harm. So, we suppress our emotions until they overwhelm us and when the temperature reaches the boiling point, improper behavior erupts.

Developing the muscular system is a process. We are not born with the ability to lift 20, 30, 40, or 50 pounds. Self-awareness is a daily activity essential for leadership growth. A new day creates a new opportunity to learn about yourself. Listen to your body, stop, and ask yourself, "Why am I upset, frustrated, crying, or anxious?" The only way to find out is to stop ignoring and start acknowledging.

Exercise

Meditate: There are areas that I have ignored, and they are underdeveloped.

Observe: Take the time to watch how I react to situations. Write down what I was feeling at the time.

Commit: Do not surpass my emotions; take inventory and ask questions. Be truthful about how I am feeling and share it with others.

DAY 5

"To be triggered is to be human. People will make you angry. You will miss the mark. People will make mistakes. You will make mistakes. It's all normal and comes with the territory of being human."
— **Susan Brady**[19]

I have been called a perfectionist; I disagree with them. I would say everything has its proper place. I would try my hardest not to make mistakes when given a task. Succeeding was few and far between, to be honest, but I would still try. I have realized that I will make mistakes, and the goal is not to keep making the same ones. I did not cry much growing up because it was not allowed. There were three things I would shed a tear for and get fussed about, however: someone talking to me harshly, when I lost something and could not find it, and when I made a mistake. Now, I can go into the reasons why these things sent me into a tailspin, but this is not a therapy session. I had to learn how to give myself grace in those areas. I am still learning to give myself grace. The problem with me holding such a high standard for myself is that I hold the same for others. I expected individuals to be on top of things and to show up ready to work. I frowned upon bringing personal situations into the workplace. I was not concerned about your dog having puppies, your sister coming to town, or your girlfriend being mad at you. The only thing I was moved by was if someone was terminally ill or had died. I was clueless about how my lack of self-awareness affected my relationship with my team, peers, and leaders.

19 Brady, S. & Susan, M. (2019). *Mastering your inner critic and 7 other high hurdles to advancement: how the best women leaders practice self-awareness to change what really matters (1st edition).* McGraw-Hill.

The discovery of the amygdala in the early 1820s by Darwin has not changed.[20] This is a small part of our brain connected to the limbic system. The amygdala connects our emotions to memory, sense, and learning. It processes what is dangerous based on what is seen and heard. If something similar occurs, the brain signals danger or produces similar emotions. We will be triggered, people will be triggered, and there is a response that comes along with it. There are other areas the amygdala affects, such as learned behavior, aggression, interpreting other's intent by how they speak or act, and emotions related to parenting. Anxiety, panic attacks, Post-traumatic stress disorder (PTSD), and phobias can harm the amygdala. If you cannot feel or sense danger, there may be some medical condition going on; I encourage you to seek a physician if this is the case for you. While it might seem reasonable to have no fear, it is not. This can cause irreplaceable damage to yourself and others.

You will get angry, and it is okay to be angry. Give yourself and others permission to express emotions. It is when we attempt to ignore our body signals that we consider making foolish mistakes. Having and expressing emotions does not give anyone the right to lash out at people. What it does is provide information on what triggers you—learning to take care of yourself by staying healthy (mentally, physically, and spiritually), eating a balanced diet, protecting yourself when you can, and giving grace (to ourselves and others). We, as humans, need to learn to give individuals the freedom to be themselves in every moment. Wearing multiple masks is taxing after a while; who wants to live like that? People are looking to follow authentic leaders.

---

20 Darwin. C. (1872). *The expression of the emotions in man and animals.*

Exercise

Meditate: Mistakes are bound to happen. Am I making the same ones?

Observe: When I make a mistake, what is my response? Do I take responsibility or blame others? How did I learn from it? When others make a mistake, what is my response?

Commit: Give grace to myself and others. Be a human being in every area of your life. Show up to your team as a person with a soul, and they will respond as human beings.

DAY 6

"You can be sure of succeeding in your attacks if you only attack places which are undefended."
— **Sun Tzu**

There are no winners in the game of hopscotch if played with others. The game is played worldwide and originated in Rome to help soldiers with their footwork. The competition is against oneself. Each person throws a rock or object to land in a square. They are to hop on one leg down and back without dropping the leg or stepping into the blocked square. On the way back, you must pick up the object and continue to the end on one foot. Who would want to play a game when there is no competition with others? As silly as it sounds, millions of children and adults play it to this day. The difference is adults need to be more balanced and keep stepping in the blocked square. The game encourages physical activity, social interaction, and creativity.

When it comes to self-awareness, the competition is also not with others. It is an inner war, and if you set out to win, balance is necessary. The balance of emotions, responsibility, accountability, grace, transparency, and honesty gets you closer to growing as a leader. Those areas that are uncovered and seen have to be dealt with. Going down, you see the object and bypass it. When returning, you are forced to deal with it by having to pick it up and finish the race. Hopscotch is not played blindfolded; the game is not meant to be tricky or unattainable. Neither is leadership growth. How effective you become is how much you are willing to attack the open places. Sun Tzu was a military general, strategist, philosopher, and writer. He is known for his militant strategies and for never losing a battle in his 40 years of leading. He stood on the state of engaging in war cautiously, for it would be a significant cost and ruinous.

Even if deciding to engage, the goal was to win, to move strategically, and to outthink the opposition.[21]

How do you know what those areas are? Continue to ask yourself, "Why?" Why am I about to speak? Will it move the conversation forward, or do I want to make myself known in the room? Do I value others' opinions, or do I do it to show that I care but will ultimately do it my way? Does the team have the same urgency I do on this matter? Why or why not? What is the pulse of the room? Why are people quiet, chatting, or unengaged? The more questions you ask, the more you will find those open spaces and allow balance to come into play. In today's society, the higher a person rises, the fewer questions they ask. The creativity of a five-year-old is just as important if not more than the responsibility given when it comes to leading others. Creativity does not mean I must give up who I am. Instead, it asks: How do I become a better version? How many different types of Vaseline lotions are there? And how many package changes? The product is "Vaseline"; all they have done is provide options and more appealing packages. Leaders spend a tremendous amount of time reinventing products and processes, but not themselves.[22] In each country, hopscotch has different variations, but the goal is still the same. Leaders must be creative in reinventing themselves, and asking questions will get them there.

Exercise

Meditate: Do not ignore those blocked spaces; expose and address them.

Observation: How many times did I want to speak when it was not necessary? Do I allow others to speak their honest opinion? If so, how? Do I ask people for their feedback on how I am doing as a member or leader of a team?

Commit: Listen to how I affect others and commit to making adjustments.

---

21 Tzu, S. (2018). *The art of war.* CreateSpace Independent Publishing
22 Gallagher, D. P., & Costal, J. (2012). *The self-aware leader: a proven model for reinventing yourself.* American Society for Training & Development.

DAY 7

Take some time today to review the past six days and write down what you have learned about yourself.

- How did these discoveries make you feel about yourself?

- Are you ready to commit to becoming a better version of yourself?

- What emotions did you recognize this week? What was happening at the time? How did you handle them?

- What response did you get from others when you were honest about your feelings? Did it free up others to open up? Have people started taking responsibility rather than pointing the finger?

- How many questions have you asked yourself this week?

Becoming self-aware is an ongoing process. Do not stop here; keep asking questions, listening, and allowing emotions to be placed appropriately. No more suppressing. Growth takes time, but when there is consistency, results are guaranteed. I do not believe anyone gets up in the morning and says they are going to harm themselves or others. However, when a person is unaware of their emotions and what is taking place around them, it can do just that—harm others unintentionally.

Leading involves taking excellent responsibility for yourself and others. You will be triggered; you are human. The goal is to recognize and acknowledge those feelings in order to address them in a healthy manner. For too long, we have had unapproachable leaders and are not sure which version of the person we will get for the day. Consistency is key to leading; people want honesty, authenticity, and transparency when wanting to be a part of something bigger than themselves. The work required involves a heart that is intentional in growing; it is through this that you will find your greatness as an effective leader.

References

Anderson, R. J., Adams, W. A., & Freeland, M. J. (2016). *Mastering leadership: An integrated framework for breakthrough performance and extraordinary business results* (1st ed.). Wiley.

Ashwell, K. (2016). *The human body atlas: How the human body works*. Quarto Publishing.

Brady, S. M. (2019). *Mastering your inner critic and 7 other high hurdles to advancement: How the best women leaders practice self-awareness to change what really matters* (1st ed.). McGraw-Hill.

Bunting, M., & Lemieux, C. (2023). *Vertical growth: How self-awareness transforms leaders and organisations*. John Wiley & Sons.

Darwin, C. (1872). *The expression of the emotions in man and animals*.

Gallagher, D. P., & Costal, J. (2012). *The self-aware leader: A proven model for reinventing yourself*. American Society for Training & Development.

Gonzalez, M. (2012). *Mindful leadership: The 9 ways to self-awareness, transforming yourself, and inspiring others* (1st ed.). Jossey-Bass.

McGaugh, J. L. (2003). *Memory and emotion: The making of lasting memories*. Columbia University Press.

Nielsen, K. E. (2009). *Beyond the miracle worker: The remarkable life of Anne Sullivan Macy and her extraordinary friendship with Helen Keller*. Beacon Press.

Norris, C. J., Chen, E. E., Zhu, D. C., Small, S. L., & Cacioppo, J. T. (2004). The interaction of social and emotional processes in the brain. *Journal of Cognitive Neuroscience, 16*(10), 1818–1829. https://doi.org/10.1162/0898929042947847

Purushothaman, R. (2021). *Emotional intelligence*. SAGE Publications India Pvt, Ltd.

Rothwell, J. (2024, February 9). Teens spend average of 4.8 hours on social media per day. *Gallup.com*. https://news.gallup.com/poll/512576/teens-spend-average-hours-social-media-per-day.aspx

Tzu, S. (2018). *The art of war*. CreateSpace Independent Publishing.

PART 3

SHINING LIGHT ON SHADOWS

"Keep your eyes on the road and both hands on the wheel. Okay, switch lanes, but do not forget to check your blind spot." I heard these words when I was learning to drive and shared them with others when I was the one doing the teaching. There is a spot where you cannot see through your peripheral vision. The only way to see the blind spot is to quickly glance over your shoulder (in the direction you want to go), and even then, you may still miss a portion of the whole picture. According to The American Academy of Ophthalmology, a blind spot starts at the back of our eye with the retina. The retina is made up of light-sensitive cells that transmit messages to our brains about what we see. There is a spot in our retina where the optic nerve connects. In these areas, there are no light-sensitive cells; this is called the "blind spot." We are usually unaware of this area because the spot is not the same in both eyes. The eye will fill in the missing areas with what it thinks should be there. Let us experiment by finding your blind spot. Take a white 3 x 5 card or a white sheet of paper. On the left side, place a dot, and on the right side, place an x (use a black marker).

Hold the paper at arm's length, at eye level, and make sure the "x" is on the right side. Close your right eye and look directly at the "x"; you can see both the "x" and the dot. Focus on the "x" and beware of the dot as you slowly bring the card closer to your face. The dot will disappear and reappear as you move it closer. Move the sheet back and forth and try to pinpoint where this occurs. Close your left eye and look at the dot. Repeat the same steps—moving the card back and forth to find the blind spot.

Take a ruler and draw a straight line from left to right in the center of each element. Now repeat the same steps as before. Does the dot or "x" disappear? There is a continuous line where the dot used to be. What is happening here is that the brain automatically fills in the blind spot with imagery around the blind spot. This happens every day of our lives, and we are unaware as we go out to view the world. Did you know we can measure our blind spot, and that each person's blind spot is different, just like our peripheral vision? Blind spots never go away, even when we take measures, such as turning our heads and looking over our shoulders.

What does this have to do with leadership? Everything. Scholars in leadership ethics, such as Bazerman and Tenbrunsel, have done extensive research along with others before them.[23] The two discovered why leaders fail to do what is right. We are unaware of our blind spots and make seemingly good excuses for why we refuse to fix problems. We see the ethical problems in government, education institutes, business, religion, and health care. Individuals have been exposed in the public eye but continue in unethical behavior.

In leadership ethics, there are heroes and villains of ethics. These heroes and villains did have something in common: they all broke the rules. Even with the heroic leaders, some unethical behavior occurred. For example, Mother Teresa had a relationship with Jesuit priest, Donald McGuire, after his convictions of child molestation. Abraham Lincoln suspended the right of habeas corpus during the Civil War. Martin Luther King Jr. broke laws: trespassing, picketing, marching without a license, and being accused of liberal conspiracy. Martin felt civil rights activists were justified in breaking "just laws." In his letter from the Birmingham jail, he wrote, "A just law is a man-made code that squares with the moral law, or the law of God. An unjust law is

---

23 Bazerman, M. H., & Tenbrunsel, A. E. (2011). *Blind spots: why we fail to do what's right and what to do about it.* Princeton University Press.

a code that is out of harmony with the moral law."[24] There are similarities between the ethical and the unethical leader when they are trying to get others to move or model their behavior for a specific outcome.

Do we intentionally set out to do something wrong even though we know what is right? Tricia was in a meeting, and a top executive instructed her not to share any information that was put out until further notice. Tricia went into another meeting where an employee asked a question she had the answer to. Tricia told the employee that more of the subject would be coming soon. Did Tricia lie, or did she tell the truth? Was it in the name of loyalty to her boss? The scenario may sound familiar, and just like Martin Luther King Jr., Tricia did what she perceived to be correct, even though she did something wrong. The blind spot of leadership is those areas where individuals make justifications for their actions because of the greater good. The brain often places imagery in place to bring clarity to a distorted area. This ethical gap between who we believe ourselves to be and who we are is called bounded awareness. Bounded awareness is the systematic failure to see information that is relevant to our personal and professional lives.[25] During this week, I want you to have an open mind to identify those blind spots and identify your biases.

---

24 King, M. (1986). *Letter from Birmingham City Jail*, in *A Testament of Hope: The Essential Writings of Martin Luther King, Jr.* ed. *James Melvin Washington, 294.* San Francisco: Harper and Row Publishers.
25 Bazerman, M. H., & Tenbrunsel, A. E. (2011). *Blind spots: why we fail to do what's right and what to do about it.* Princeton University Press.

DAY 1

"The easiest way to solve a problem is to deny it exists."
— **Isaac Asimov**

If only we could solve problems by ignoring them. Having blind spots affects decision-making. Leaders being aware of those blind spots can help solve issues rather than ignore them. As mentioned in the opening of the chapter, we all have blind spots and our brains will fill in information that is not there. How can a person get accurate information when it comes to blind spots? Joseph Luft and Harry Ingham developed the Johari Window model in 1955.[26] The Johari window has four quadrants: Known to all (arena)—the information is known by all parties; Known to others (blind spots)—others have and observe information about me, but I am not aware; Known to me (facade)—I know things about myself but withhold this information from others, leaving others with an impression that is not entirely accurate; Unknown (unconscious)—an area that is not known to any of us at this time.

---

26 Luft, J. and Ingram, H. (1955, 1970). *The Johari window, a graphic model of interper-sonal awareness.*

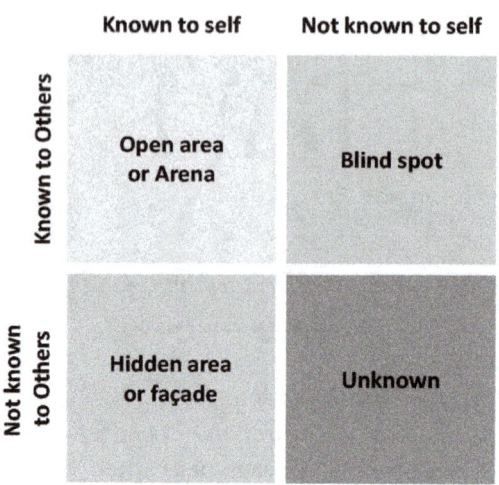

	Known to self	**Not known to self**
Known to Others	Open area or Arena	Blind spot
Not known to Others	Hidden area or façade	Unknown

The Johari Window Model

In Luft and Ingham's discovery, the Johari Window provides a picture of seeking feedback, gaining new insights and awareness into oneself, and risking exposing parts of ourselves to peers, subordinates, and supervisors to reduce the facade and develop the authentic self that is known to self and others with ease.[27] The blind spot in the model refers to what is known to others but unaware to self. For example, when speaking, you rub your pointer finger and thumb together, say "Umm" every other word, or lick your lips constantly. You would only be aware of this if there were some feedback; once you receive the information, you take measures to change. Some individuals choose to keep their blind spots. They refuse to be open to what others have to share about their behavior on a particular matter. Blind spots are not a permanent human element that cannot be resolved. Blindness is a condition of being unable to see or lacking perception, awareness, or discernment, according to Merriam-Webster.[28] The blind spot is a particular place. In

27 McLean, Pamela. (2012). *The Completely Revised Handbook of Coaching: A Developmental Approach.* John Wiley & Sons, Incorporated.
28 "blindness." 2023. In Merriam-Webster.com. Retrieved November 4, 2023, from https://www.merriam-webster.com/dictionary/blindess

leadership, blind spots are where a person's view is obstructed. They do not want to or refuse to see another viewpoint. This is pragmatic as a leader when you cannot make adjustments and change. This is the reason why most organizations are behind the times: no knowledge sharing, no succession planning, no new processes, no new tools, no new team membership, or no new products.

Karen Blakley says that a blind spot is a regular tendency to repress, distort, dismiss, or fail to notice information, views, or ideas in a particular area that results in an individual failing to learn, change, or grow in response to changes in that area.[29] So, it is not just about a lack of knowledge; it is also about not wanting to hear feedback or pretending something is not or did not happen. There is a gap between who we think we are and who we truly are. The only way to close this gap is by asking for feedback and taking action to change. Dealing with blind spots means addressing the root causes: fear, anxiety, disappointments, or rejection. As a leader, you may be good in one area but must improve in another. By continuing to pretend, you are putting the team and the organization in jeopardy. This is a result of fear of someone else taking the lead position. Leading effectively is based on something other than technical skills; ask Steve Jobs. How you treat others is the key.

Exercise

Meditate: I have blind spots; I must be intentional about closing the gap.

Observe: What is my response when others point out how I address or do not address a situation?

Commit: Ask for feedback from peers, subordinates, and supervisors regularly.

---

29 Blakeley, Karen. (2007). *Leadership blind spots-- and what to do about them.* Jossey-Bass.

DAY 2

"I'm sometimes asked, 'When will there be enough?' and my answer is, 'When there are nine.' People are shocked. But there'd been nine men, and nobody's ever raised a question about that."
— **Ruth Bader Ginsburg**

We do not think anything is wrong when we can only see through our lenses. Why would anyone think having nine men on the Supreme Court is wrong? The worldview of how our society is supposed to run, gender roles, family dynamics, religious practices, organizational culture, and political agendas does not allow for the unseen to be seen. I am still amazed at how, after all these years of progression in our laws, we still have a gender pay gap. Is it because we refuse to see what has been unseen? Our country has allowed for stagnation, treating only some human beings equally because of fearfully dismissing information. Ruth Bader Ginsburg was the second female appointed to the Supreme Court justice. For three years, when O'Connor retired in 2006 until Sonia Sotomayor was appointed in 2009, she was the only female. Still, in the history of the Supreme Court Justice, there have been 114 members, and 110 of them have been men. In her life, Ruth Bader Ginsburg fought for the equality of women in both her personal and professional life—the three things that she said were stacked against her: being Jewish, being a woman, and being a mom.[30]

Today, we would not see these three things as an issue to lead and work in a field in which a person is passionate. It is not a problem, but we still have to endure those struggles to exist in

---

30 Justice Ruth Bader Ginsburg. The Library of Congress. (n.d.). https://www.loc.gov/item/2022630265/

a world that does not see everyone on an equal playing field. When dealing with blind spots, a leader may accept the facts they have but refuse to take action to eliminate those areas. Research shows that most leaders are typically ten years or more outdated from their industry. They are behind in the market and waste money hiring consultants when given the root causes and possible solutions. They refuse to go forth outside of what they are accustomed to. A leader can become complacent when the organization is doing well. There is no longer a passion for the industry; the leader is simply maintaining the business. The problem with keeping the organization functioning is that changes are happening that could be more feasible. The world is complex and forever changing; it teaches us that no person can monopolize the truth.[31]

Blind spots exist in all situations, and how individuals perceive unknown information, can have both positive and negative effects. Science can be a wonder and reality. The most profound motivation for doing science is the sense of wonder that arises naturally when confronted with the intricacies of the natural world. Within the face of so much uncertainty, Einstein posed a question: Is uncertainty an intrinsic part of reality or merely a feature of our current description of the world?[32] Leaders have to be able to see the world not only through their lenses but through the lenses of others. We miss out on the bigger picture when we can only see through our lenses. How many times have you said or are saying that if management would just listen? They are not the ones doing the work every day! Employees can raise signs and march around buildings, yet leaders will still be unable to see or hear them due to their blind spots, unless they are willing to change their lenses.

---

31 Blakeley, Karen. (2007). *Leadership blind spots-- and what to do about them.* Jossey-Bass.
32 Byers, W. (2011). *The Blind Spot: Science and the Crisis of Uncertainty.* Princeton University Press.

Exercise

Meditate: The world is a wonder and I am unable to see it all from where I sit.

Observe: How do I respond when others tell me the idea will not work?

Commit: Listen, observe, ask for feedback, and take action to adjust. See the world in its wonder and the perception of reality.

DAY 3

Who sets out to become an ineffective leader? We are all good leaders with biases until we decide not to become good leaders. We make daily decisions about whether we choose to become influential leaders. You picking up this book and reading it is a sign you desire to connect with your team on a deeper level. You take training, read articles, work hard, and care deeply for others—all for what? You are willing to make adjustments to better meet the team's needs. You are even willing to see and do what is uncomfortable to succeed. In all those efforts, you must be consciously aware of those unseen areas others can see.

The lack of awareness hinders productivity and growth in organizations. Philosophers call human beings "native realists"; they believe what they see is the plain truth.[33] We have mental models that agree with this as well. However, Dr. Sterman challenges our thoughts by telling us all models are wrong. Models are built on our experiences, and experiences are different for everyone. They give us a reference point in what we believe to be true. Suppose I had terrible experiences with public transportation. I would think public transportation is inadequate and try to dissuade others from using it.

On the other hand, Chelsea likes transportation and does not see a problem. For the record, I am for public transportation.

---

33 Sterman, J. D. (2002, pg 501-531). *All models are wrong: reflections on becoming a systems scientist, 18 (4).* System Dynamics Review.

This example shows the misconception of truth we tend to possess. We get into conflicts with no resolve thanks to our models of truth. Have you been or do you know of a time when individuals disagreed and both presented facts and good viewpoints, each concluding that their point was accurate and complete?

Those biases leave us in the facade window wearing a mask and unwilling to uncover what is unknown. You, however, are willing to uncover the unknown, or you would not be reading this. Leaders typically tend to fall victim to having biases in the following areas:

- Everyone needs to meet my standards.
- Those I hired are more qualified to do the work than the ones inherited.
- I include my team when making decisions.
- I am a good listener.
- I know how to delegate.
- Work your way up.
- I am open and honest.

You may have excellent standards, and there is nothing wrong with having them. Make sure the criteria you have for others are realistic and meet the needs of what is required in the organization. You could expect others to have the same drive and passion (work overtime), have the same academic status, or take little time off because you do not take off regularly. You include the team but focus on specific individuals or whoever may get to you first. You delegate but only those things that do not have awareness in the organization. You started where they were and expect them to take the same route to get a promotion. You share information but require unrealistic processes to receive it. Truly understanding those blind spots is being aware that your mental model of truth is wrong without a complete picture.

The only way to conquer those blind spots is by sharing information. Listen when others come to disclose a facade you have about yourself. People do not easily disregard their be-liefs.[34] Learning together can help bridge the gap between what is false reality and what is reality. Change is painful but doable. In the Western culture, we have yet to learn as a culture to think deeply and take time to reflect.[35] We are quick to move on our agendas and timelines. To come to the truth is to pause in the present.

Exercise

Meditate: My model of what is reality is not complete.

Observe: How do I take in work and delegate? How do I view my team or others who do not have the same work ethic?

Commit: Share information, pause, reflect, learn, and do not judge others on their views.

---

34 Blakeley, Karen. (2007). *Leadership blind spots-- and what to do about them.* Jossey-Bass.

35 Geisler, J. (2023, pg 38-39). *Beware 7 blind spots and biases.* Healthcare Financial Management, 77(4).

DAY 4

"The lies the government and media tell are amplifications of the lies we tell ourselves. To stop being conned, stop conning yourself."
—James Wolcott

You should not think too highly of yourself. Wisdom tells us that if you are to be praised, let others do the praising—not because you are looking for validation, but because there is a window you cannot see. How do we truly see ourselves only through the eyes of others? How do you know if there is sauce on the side of your mouth? There are two scenarios: one, someone is nice enough to tell you, or two, you go to the bathroom and see it in the mirror. How often has someone told you something is on your face, and you did not attempt to remove it? Probably when you were being stubborn or trying to prove a point. Is the point worth it when you are still walking around with gunk on your face?

We tend to believe the false impression we have told ourselves rather than face the hidden, blind, and even unknown spots. It is no longer a secret once it is brought to your attention. The question is, what do you do with the information now that it is revealed? Let's take the previous example: do you acknowledge the food is there and refuse to remove it because of the source or place? Pride will hinder you from reaching your goals to becoming an effective leader. Why would someone take the time to tell you about something on your face and not have a genuine concern about your well-being? Pride will tell you they could have waited, told you another way or only in private, or simply waited until the meal was over. No, you have something restricting others from seeing your qualities, and you would rather them see the facade. Pride goes before destruction and leads to unhealthy conflict, disgrace, and humiliation; it will make you believe you have credentials and they do not so you are in a higher status. As leaders, we must live in harmony with others and humble ourselves. We should live our lives not to impress others but to humbly think of others.

Society's norms tell us that we must act and behave in a certain way to achieve success, but those measurements come from a place of misplaced mindset of self-gratification, such as patting yourself on the back, giving yourself a high five, putting yourself up for awards, taking credit for selfish gain or work you did not do, and looking for ways to excel. Of course, we are to encourage ourselves and recognize the skills we bring to the table. We are speaking in terms of puffing up ourselves to be seen and heard and not thinking of others. Leadership is all about influencing and serving others. Pride will cause a great fall. We have seen this over and over again throughout history. I am still perplexed at how individuals believe they will get away with grievous behavior; everything will come to light. There was a song called "Don't Believe the Hype" by Public Enemy. The song came out during a time when people believed everything the media was putting out: race, communities, politics, and economic makeup. The song's message is to not believe everything you see and hear, think for yourself, go and discover for yourself, and use critical thinking. People were being wrongfully accused of crimes and being convicted due to racial profiling. We know there is a long history of that in our country. During this time, the media had a significant influence, considering they could reach people in a matter of seconds on an issue, and people took it as facts rather than a subset of information with areas unknown.

Wolcott is saying there are unknown areas, and once you have all the facts, you will know the truth. We have convinced ourselves to believe a false reality rather than look in the mirror and gather information for ourselves. You don't have to remain in a place of unawareness, lacking perception, or unable to see. Is pride blind? Yes.

Exercise

Meditate: All information is not facts; it is information to continue to seek out truth.

Observe: How do I listen to others?

Commit: Take in all information, assess, and gather more to come to clarity.

DAY 5

"The eyes do not see what the mind does not want"
— D.H. Lawrence

Our experiences, knowledge, and understanding are how we see. To see clearly is not only a scientific process but also an intellectual one. The more we read and dig for information, the more discoveries we make. Inventions are made based on exploring new information in existing areas. We do not see through our eyes; sight comes from the visual cortex. Our eyes capture light from objects around us and transmit that information to our brains. Our eyes are not aligned, and there is a space without images or light. What does this mean? We are all blind somewhere along the line. This type of blindness is curable.

When you are not willing to put in the effort, nothing will come out. Results will not fall from the sky, and you will not wake up the next day and—BAAM—change. The work you put in is the work you will get out. We are blinded by our ignorance of failing to dig for the truth, or saying history tells it all. I remember watching a documentary about the Appalachian people known as the "Children of the Mountains" several years ago. The show told their story of living with limited resources, but they made it work in the modern world. One particular issue that kept coming up was their dental hygiene. Because the area was hard to get to, they needed a dentist in the town. Once a month, a mobile dentist truck would come and provide dental care. Mountain Dew was destroying their teeth; most of them were rotten, yet it was still available for them to purchase. They would drink cases of it per day and even give it to their babies. In the 1950s, there were ads featuring a mother giving the baby 7-Up and instructions on how much to add to the baby's milk. With newfound information, this method is highly discouraged, and dental hygienists have expressed this information to the Appalachians. Shockingly, twenty-six percent of preschoolers in the region have tooth decay, and fifteen percent of 18 to 24-year-olds have had a tooth extracted because of tooth decay or erosion. Despite this, they continue to drink Mountain Dew. [36]

Here, it is. Even with new information and instructions on what not to do, the behavior continues. This behavior is no different from how we treat leadership. Reports have been shared based on research, yet we tend to unconsciously overlook blind spots in our organization. There is never a problem until there is a problem. William is a consistent employee who does good work, comes in on time, communicates with his supervisor and peers, and is well-rounded. Over time, William has come in late, missed deadlines, and has not been talkative. One day, there is a call that someone is on the roof of the building; it is William, ready to end his life. Okay, you are saying this is extreme. Yes, it is, but it is also a fact. There were signs, and those signs were ignored because his leaders refused to see them. To see is to address the situation. The leader would have had to have a conversation with William about his behavior change and taken time out of their schedule to reach William and get to the root of the problem. Situations don't have to become extreme problems. They do because we refuse to address those blind spots.

Exercise

Meditate: What I am willing to learn, I am able to see.

Observe: How much do I search for truth?

Commit: Seek out the truth before responding. Be willing to put in the work to get the results I want.

---

36 Keefe, S. E. (2000). *Mountain Identity and the Global Society in a Rural Appalachian County.*

DAY 6

"Change starts with our beliefs."
—Jim Haudan & Rich Berens

In the late 1800s, we believed in giving people, even children, cocaine to ease a toothache. Cocaine was used as a local anesthetic. The dentist would apply cocaine to numb the area and would extract the teeth. It was not until the 1900s that cocaine started to be banned, and Novocaine became the preferred local anesthetic. At the time, society believed cocaine was good for individuals until more research was done to discover it was harmful instead. Below, you will see advertisements and products sold to the public. The cure for disease in those days caused more harm; morphine, cocaine, and alcohol were the common ingredients. During those times, there were no checks and balances; people could spend good money on advertisements because the people believed whatever was put out in the press or marketing. As obscure as this may be, people did not challenge so-called "experts"; they took everything as facts.

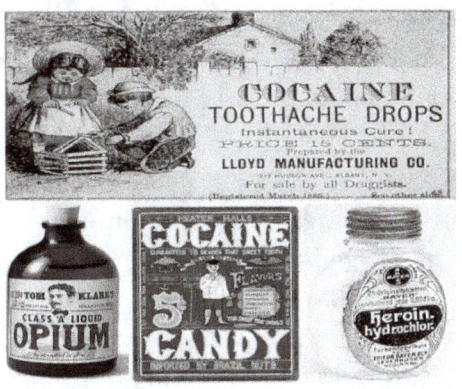

Accountability is vital to closing the gap on blind spots. When driving, you are accountable to others on the road, insurance companies, and the Department of Motor Vehicles. If you mess up in one or more of these areas, it will make you aware of the responsibilities of being a licensed driver. If you want to keep driving, you will adjust. Leading requires accountability. Who have you made yourself accountable to other than your supervisor? It should not be a person who will only tell you the good things and agree with your conduct. You need someone who will challenge your motives, behaviors, thinking, and heart.

Haudan and Berens have been in the corporate world for over 30 years and have seen our society's different eras. They believe leaders are still leading as though we are in the Industrial Age when, in fact, we are in the Information Age and Experience Economy.[37] People still want to work but they want to be a part of something bigger than themselves. They want money, more of it, and less work. Leaders are aware but continue in the dinosaur's way of leading. This is why we see the "great" leaders in all the awe and glory. Leading effectively should be a norm, not few and far between.

Dealing with those blind spots will enhance our organization and economy. According to the Gallup survey from 30 years ago through today, engagement has not changed. Thirty percent are engaged, twenty percent are actively disengaged, and fifty percent are indifferent. This shows leadership needs to make the necessary adjustments to grow effectively. Every leader should look for ways to make the required adjustments to change these numbers. Lisa Earl McLeod, author, speaker, and consultant, said work is hard and competitive, but it should not suck out your soul.

Change starts in the heart, and it begins with the leadership. It is not the fault of employees if they are disengaged.

---

37 Haudan, J. & Berens, R. (2018.). *What are your blind spots: Conquering the 5 misconceptions that hold leaders back.* McGraw.

Exercise

Meditate: Change starts with me as a leader.

Observe: How is my heart? What changes have I made?

Commit: See what is working, what is not working, and get input from my team to make adjustments on a regular basis.

DAY 7

Take some time today to reflect on what you've learned during the past six days.

- What blind spots have you discovered?
- Do you have an accountability partner?
- Have you asked for feedback from others? Do you agree with their assessment?
- What are you committed to doing to address those blind spots?

The first step to making any change is acknowledgment. Bravo for acknowledging you have blind spots. Do not try to tackle them all at once. Take the time to unpack each one separately. Here are five steps to narrow the gap:

1. Recognize your vulnerability to your unconscious biases. If you find yourself thinking, "I will never do that," be aware of making those moral decisions and making sure your self-interest is not included.

2. Plan appropriately and reflect objectively and honestly on your behavior. What motivates you? Thinking about your motivations helps eliminate self-wants before making a decision.

3. Think analytically before you act.

4. Publicly commit to a decision. People who tend to commit publicly will follow through with the decision more often than others who do not.[38]

---

38 Brockner, J. & Rubin, J. Z. (1985). *Entrapment in escalating conflicts: A social psychological analysis.* Springer-Verlag.

5. Would you tell your parent(s) or someone you highly respect what you did—no filters? If not, then you are still in the self-interest and facade window. We do not want people that we hold in high regard to think less of us.

When looking at the Johari Window, stay out of the facade and blind spots window. As you grow, these two windows should become smaller over time, and the "known to self and known to others" should get more comprehensive to the point it is no longer a window but a door.

We all have blind spots; there is no way around that. Listening to others about what they see and what we believe about ourselves is different. You may think you are a good communicator, but others believe you leave out important information. You think you delegate and allow others to lead, while others say you are a micro manager or controlling. Take time to observe and ask the hard questions if you are ready to change and stay in the mirror.

References

Bazerman, M. H., & Tenbrunsel, A. E. (2011). *Blind spots: Why we fail to do what's right and what to do about it*. Princeton University Press.

Blakeley, K. (2007). *Leadership blind spots—and what to do about them*. Jossey-Bass.

Blindness. (2023). In *Merriam-Webster.com*. Retrieved November 4, 2023, from https://www.merriam-webster.com/dictionary/blindness

Brockner, J., & Rubin, J. Z. (1985). *Entrapment in escalating conflicts: A social psychological analysis*. Springer-Verlag.

Byers, W. (2011). *The blind spot: Science and the crisis of uncertainty*. Princeton University Press.

Delgado, M. F., Nguyen, N. T., Cox, T. A., Singh, K., Lee, D. A., Dueker, D. K., ... & Samples, J. R. (2002). Automated perimetry: A report by the American Academy of Ophthalmology. *Ophthalmology, 109*(12), 2362-2374.

Geisler, J. (2023). Beware 7 blind spots and biases. *Healthcare Financial Management, 77*(4), 38–39.

Haudan, J., & Berens, R. (2018). *What are your blind spots: Conquering the 5 misconceptions that hold leaders back*. McGraw-Hill.

Justice Ruth Bader Ginsburg. The Library of Congress. (n.d.). https://www.loc.gov/item/2022630265/

Keefe, S. E. (2000). Mountain identity and the global society in a rural Appalachian county.

King, M. L., Jr. (1986). Letter from Birmingham City Jail. In J. M. Washington (Ed.), *A testament of hope: The essential writings of Martin Luther King, Jr.* (pp. 294–). Harper and Row Publishers.

Luft, J., & Ingram, H. (1955). The Johari window, a graphic model of interpersonal awareness. Luft, (1970).

McLean, P. (2012). *The completely revised handbook of coaching: A developmental approach.* John Wiley & Sons.

Sterman, J. D. (2002). All models are wrong: Reflections on becoming a systems scientist. *System Dynamics Review, 18*(4), 501–531.

PART 4

FOLLOW THE LEADER

Leaders don't like the idea of being a follower. However, a leader is not separate from a follower. They are two sides of the same coin. If you are a leader and have to answer to anyone, you are a follower. Both roles are interchangeable with one another. While there are not centuries of research on followership as there are on leadership, the interest and how important this area is to effective leadership has piqued the interest of many. The only thing I heard in the Armed Forces about following was that if you want to lead, you must first learn to follow. We are set to believe leading is powerful and following is weak, but neither is weak. In fact, it takes courage to follow. Followers can empower their leaders and leaders can empower their followers. One cannot exist without the other.

Organizations spends thousands of dollars on leadership training and development for those who are in leadership positions. There is rarely any formal or set training for followers. Employees are researching other ways to get the necessary training to develop themselves. One downfall that we must all overcome is how we view followership. We have been taught to agree with our leaders and not to go against what they say. We have too many yes-people rather than those who will challenge ideas, concepts, procedures, or decisions. We are afraid that if we speak out, it will come back to bite us; we'll be shunned, black-balled, looked over, or viewed as challenging authority. Either way, organizations need leaders who welcome thoughts and insight and adhere to warnings if they hear a decision going south.

The landscape has improved but could still use some more grooming in this area. People have said they do not wish to be leaders and prefer being followers. They enjoy being number two instead of one and would like for others to understand the importance of the other numbers on the team. I can agree! A basketball team roster consists of 12 players, and there can only be five players on the court at all times. Each player has a role and a strength on the team. You need someone to pass the ball, get it from one end to the other, block shots, and defend opponents. And then, there is one person, not two or ten, but one, who makes the shot. The credit is given to the person who made the shot, but they would have never made it without the help of the others. Not wanting to lead or follow is not bad. It is a choice. No matter the choice, be effective. There are times when you must be able to recognize when to lead and when to follow.

According to Riggo and based on the 1998 Kellerman model, there are five different styles of followership (Riggo, 2008).[39]

1. The Sheep: Sheep are passive. They wait for the leader to tell them what to do and how. They want the leader to do all the thinking and motivate them.

2. Yes-People: Yes-people are positive. They are on board with the leader and are full of energy. They believe the job of thinking and providing direction belongs to the leader. They will complete a task, come back, and ask what is next.

3. The Alienated: The alienated see themselves as the loner. They can think for themselves and they have energy, but it is more negative than positive. They are the only ones who will challenge decisions that are being made.

4. The Pragmatics: The pragmatics are not the first out people. They are the ones who will get on board when they figure out where the boat is going. They will wait things out.

5. The Stars: The star follower is active, motivated, a thinker, a challenger, and has high energy. They will offer ideas and solutions and challenge decisions to get the leader(s) to look at other alternatives before coming to a definitive decision. People see them as leaders in disguise, but they are followers who want the best for everyone involved. Leaders see them as the "go-to" person.

It is important to identify the difference between the types of followers and how they think when it comes to roles and responsibilities. Leaders make decisions on whether to follow

39 Kellerman B. (2008). *Followership: How Followers are Creating Change and Changing Leaders.* Harvard Business School Publishing.

the call. Followers make decisions on what to follow. There are no leaders without followers and no followers without leaders. Followers need leaders to teach them, show them, and receive new insights and discoveries. There are things the leader can see and can reveal to the followers. Followers are to be like disciplined disciples. Disciples are in the position of learning and are not afraid to admit what they do not know. The leader is there teaching and sharing information at all times. They allow followers to discover and come to their own conclusions. Neither has their ego or set agendas; both are looking toward a common goal and shared interest. Followers need to let their leaders know what they need to learn, while the leader needs to continue to learn to teach the followers.

Followership is about doing the right things in any given situation. Followership is no different than leadership in terms of behaving ethically and morally as the situation requires. Followers are to say the right things, do the right things in the right way, and be accountable and responsible. Response-able action means having a sense of purpose and acting with propriety. This is an ancient meaning of decorum, having a renewed identity through change. The four cardinal virtues involve how followers' behaviors are effective: prudence, justice, fortitude, and temperance. Living a life of virtue is an inner fulfillment that fights against human nature to do what is pleasing to self even if it harms others. Virtues are not just ideas. They are practices that must be learned.[40]

In 2023, Patterson developed a model where the foundation is virtue-based. Overall, it is love that is foundational for leadership. There is a type of love, social, or moral sense that must be present to lead and follow. Through love, trust is built and it needs to flow in both directions.[41]

---

40 Kellerman B. (2008). *Followership: How Followers are Creating Change and Changing Leaders.* Harvard Business School Publishing.
41 Crowther, S. (2018). *Biblical Servant Leadership: An Exploration of Leadership for the Contemporary Context.* Springer International Publishing.

The leader considers the needs of the follower by looking at each person with unique qualities and needs.[42] If the leader is trustworthy, they can inspire trust in the follower. The leader and the follower have a constant interchange of serving one another. There is humility, patience, kindness, and gentleness when individuals serve one another. Leaders recognize their shortcomings and followers recognize theirs. This allows for both parties to see one another's humanity and work toward a shared goal. As we have moved into a new era of how we work, how we view followers and the contributions they bring to organizations is changing. Leaders are expecting more, followers want to give more, and organizations are demanding more. Followership involves individuals who engage while interacting with leaders to meet organizational objectives.[43] Over the week, we will look at the different ways followers are impacting the future of organizations. Remember, followership and leadership are not stand-alone roles.

---

42 Patterson, K. A. (2003). *Servant leadership: A theoretical model.* Paper presented at the servant leadership roundtable.
43 Lapierre, L. M., & Carstein, M. K. (Eds.) (2014). *Followership: what is it and why do people follow? (First edition.).* Emerald.

DAY 1

"He who cannot be a good follower, cannot be a good leader"
— **Aristotle**

What is followership? Why do people follow? There have been over 170 years of research on leadership and 35 years of research on followership. There is a 135-year difference between the two. There has almost been a negative connotation attached to being a follower. Growing up, I would often hear , "Be a leader, be different, stand out, or do not follow. You set the course." After hearing this tune over and over again, you would believe there is something wrong with becoming a follower. When leadership is discussed or defined, the followers are part, if not the main ingredient, of leadership; influencing **others**, developing **others**, serving **others**, and directing **others**. Who are the **others**? They are followers, the ones who help advance the organization's goals.

Bligh says there has been little interest and research into really understanding followership.[44] Scholars, such as Zaleznik, did a typology of followers in 1965 to help leaders understand their followers and for followers to learn how to become leaders[45] and discovered that on a horizontal axis, one end initiates those who are withdrawn. On the vertical axis, leaders control those who want to be controlled by their leaders. The models display four types of followers; withdrawn, masochistic, compulsive, and impulsive. Zaleznik was trained in psychoanalytic

---

44 Bligh, M. C. (2011, pg 1180 -1216). *Followership and follower-centered approaches.* In A. Bryman, K. Grint, B. Jackson, M. Uhl-Bien, & D. Collinson (Eds.), The sage handbook of leadership.
45 Northouse, P. G. (2019). *Leadership: theory and practice (Eighth edition.).* SAGE.

theory where the types are based on psychological concepts.[46] Kelley, who wrote an article for the Harvard Business Review in 1988 titled "In Praise of Followers" and another in 1992 titled "The Power of Followership," developed the five types of followership model.[47] [48] Chaleff, Yukl & Van Fleet, Hollander, Collinson, Shamir, Uhl-Bien, Riggio, Lowe, and Carsten have all done extensive work on the subject of followership. They have brought to society the idea that followership is not a negative position to be in; there is power in following. The "Never to Follow" model was pushed on people, giving examples of leaders who had great influence but used it in a negative manner. Adolf Hitler used his leadership to commit genocide and initiated World War II. Warren Jeff used religion to rape, molest, and alienate people from society. Joseph Vissarionovich Stalin killed over 20 million people under his leadership. Mao Zedong killed 78 million people under his rule. King Leopold II and Pol Pot are also prime examples of leaders using their influence in negative ways. There can be a debate on whether these individuals are leaders. They had great influence; people followed their lead in carrying out what was asked of them. Some people follow blindly, but some follow with an engaging heart to serve the common good.

There is never a time when a leader is not a follower. Research has shown that followers are not weak, gullible, or desperate for validation from leaders.[49] Followers are courageous and challenge the status quo when it comes to meeting objectives. Webster defines a follower as a person who moves behind someone or something.[50] The synonym that is often used for followers is "subordinate," and is still often used today. In many leadership books around the early 2000s, the word "follower" in the index says, *see subordinate*. There are other terms used, such as "direct

46 Northouse, P. G. (2019). *Leadership: theory and practice (Eighth edition.)*. SAGE.
47 Kelley, R. (1988, pg 142-148). *In praise of followers*. Harvard Business Review 66(6).
48 Kelley, R. (1992). *The Power of Followership*. New York: Doubleday.
49 Lapierre, L. M., & Carstein, M. K. (Eds.) (2014). *Followership: what is it and why do people follow? (First edition.)*. Emerald.
50 "follower." 2023. In Merriam-Webster.com. Retrieved November 14, 2023, from https://www.merriam-webster.com/dictionary/loyalty

reports," that distinguish the difference between someone who is under a leader's direct authority versus someone who follows in the absence of a formal authority relationship.

Here are some definitions gathered by Crossman & Crossman in their study on *Followership*.[51]

Definition	Author
Attaining one's individual goals by being influenced by a leader into participating in individual or group efforts toward organizational goals in a given situation. Followership thereby becomes seen as a function of the follower, the leader, and situational variables.	*(Wortman, 1982)*
People who are effective in the follower role have the vision to see both the forest and the trees, the social capacity to work well with others, the strength of character to flourish without heroic status, the moral and psychological balance to pursue personal and corporate goals at no cost to others, and, above all, the desire to participate in a team effort for the accomplishment of some greater common purpose.	*(Kelley, 1988)*
A process in which subordinates recognize their responsibility to comply with the orders of leaders and take appropriate action consistent with the situation to carry out those orders to the best of their ability. In the absence of orders, they estimate the proper action to contribute to mission performance and take that action.	*(Townsend and Gebhart, 1997)*
Subordinates who have less power, authority, and influence than do their superiors and who therefore usually, but not invariably, fall into line.	*(Kellerman, 2008)*

---

51 Crossman, B. & Crossman, J. (2011). *Conceptualizing followership – a review of the literature.* Leadership 7(4). 481–49. Sage. doi: 10.1177/1742715011416891.

Followers do leadership, not followership. And while followers sometimes change places and become leaders, they do have to be leaders to exert influence, to use power resources to persuade others of their position. In sum, followers are active agents in the leadership relationship, not passive recipients of the leader's influence	*(Rost, 1995)*
A relational role in which followers have the ability to influence leaders and contribute to the improvement and attainment of group and organizational objectives. It is primarily a hierarchically upwards influence.	*(Carsten et al., 2010)*

Throughout history, you will see how the role is seen as shifting from one of being under authority to one of being in a relationship with leadership, influencing the outcomes of the leader and the organization. Not all followers follow in a way that is considered "normal" in our culture. Although we are in the early stages of taking a closer look at followership, some things are certain. Nothing can be accomplished without a relationship. Both leadership and followership have certain characteristics attached to them. Additionally, leaders are not effective without being effective followers.

Exercise

Meditate: A good follower is a good leader.

Observe: How do I respond to authority? Look at other stories of different leaders and followers.

Commit: Work in humility knowing that I will always be a follower.

DAY 2

"World is full of followers and leaders, and I think that if one can become both and be both, to follow in order to lead, and to lead in order to follow, then I think you're on the right path."
— **George Ogilvie**

We spend too much time placing limitations on things. Does the world only have enough room for a certain number of followers and a certain number of leaders? We are all leaders and followers; it depends on the circumstances in which role we will play. If we concluded that we are both, sayings like, "I was told to do it", "This is for the senior leadership to decide", "I don't have a say", and "What do you want me to do next?", would go away, never to be heard of again! There has been little research done on followership that introduced a typology of followership.[52] The most common typology referred to is one Kelley developed. Kelley believed followers are the most valuable asset to an organization and they go unrecognized. He looked at the motivations and behaviors of followers.[53] Chaleff's typology looked at the roles of the followers in the leadership process.[54] He was motivated by the actions of World War II and how individuals would carry out horrific crimes against other human beings.[55] How could this be prevented? Followers should share a common purpose and goal to follow rather than just serving the leader.

In Chaleff's view, followers have to be morally strong. They are to do the right things at the right times and not carry out orders

52 Zaleznik A. (1965, pg 119-131). *The dynamics of subordinacy.* Harvard Business Review 43(3): 119–131.
53 Kelley, R. (1992). *The Power of Followership.* New York: Doubleday.
54 Chaleff I. (2008, pg 67-87). *Creating new ways of following.* In: Riggio R, Chaleff I and Lipman-Blument J (eds)The Art of Followership: How Great Followers Create Great Leaders and Organizations. Jossey-Bass.
55 Northouse, P. G. (2019). *Leadership: theory and practice (Eighth edition.).* SAGE.

because they were told. Followers need the courage to challenge leaders and the courage to support them. If not, ethical abuse takes place. Followers are to assume responsibility, support the organization, challenge the leaders if the common goal is being threatened, and champion the need for change when necessary. You may be thinking, "I will be canceled if I challenge my leadership or be retaliated against." In some cases, yes, this could happen, but there are silver linings. You can see there are no longer common grounds. I once worked with a colleague who was in a situation in which leadership was not taking into consideration what others were saying and they were continually being sacrificed for the cause. I recommended they stay and deal with it or go and find employment elsewhere. I believe some individuals take their power and authority and use it for personal gain rather than for the benefit of others. If people don't stand up to those behaviors, they will continue. Now, there could be other considerations in a situation. In those cases, other measures might be necessary. You may need to consult Human Resources, Ethics, the Ombudsman, or the Equal Employment Office.

Followership ought to be a bottom-up approach rather than a top-down one. In doing so, it keeps both parties accountable for one another's behaviors. When we look at followership there are three distinctive groups; *descriptive*—actual behavior, *prescriptive*—behaviors that should be exhibited, and *situational*—how the leader and follower interact based on the situation.[56] Each group is based on a choice of how the follower and leader decide to behave, from a self-state or selfless state.

Exercise

Meditate: If I am a leader, I am a follower.

Observe: How do I use my authority? Is it in an ethical way? Am I selfish or selfless?

Commit: Be both a leader and a follower. I am not the only one with authority. *I am under authority.*

---

56 Crossman, B. & Crossman, J. (2011). *Conceptualizing followership—a review of the literature.* Leadership 7(4). 481–49. Sage. doi: 10.1177/1742715011416891.

DAY 3

"Don't initiate! Follow the initiator! Follow the follower."
— **Viola Spolin**

There are times when we allow our ego to get in the way of becoming who we are. An ego will tell us we are more, that we have given more so we deserve more, know more, and all should know it was me and not them. Egos produce toxic environments.[57] Viola Spolin is the originator of theater plays. She was passionate about the work. She believed if there was a problem, there was a game to solve it; if it did not exist, then you needed to create one.[58] Following was a way to get out of your head and retract your upbringing and past experiences. The goal was to be in the moment with those at the moment. She would argue that people want to get their names out there, steal others' work, and never fully understand the foundation of the work. She did not want you to praise her for her work. The thank you would be in the results, and it was a way to keep her ego at bay. In the theater, some came to play, and some came to steal.

In followership, you have to be mindful of the ego; we all have them. Kellerman introduced the levels of engagement of followers through her experience as a scientist: isolate, bystander, participant, activist, and diehard.[59] *Isolates* are completely disengaged. They are detached from the organization, leader, and others, and do not care. This behavior leads to giving

57 Gaunt, D. (2022). *Ego and Authority. In Ego, Authority, Failure.* BookBaby.
58 Aretha Sills with Carol Sills. (Nov, 2023). *Viola Spolin Biography.* https://www.violaspolin.org/bio
59 Kellerman B. (2008). *Followership: How Followers are Creating Change and Changing Leaders.* Harvard Business School Publishing.

leaders more power and it can backfire. *Bystanders* are sitting back, watching, and not participating. They are aware of what is happening around them but choose not to get involved. *Participants* are partially engaged; they are willing to challenge and stand up to the leader on certain issues. *Activists* have a strong opinion about the leader's policies and will act on their own beliefs. They are considered "Change Agents." Lastly, *Diehards* are engaged extremely. They are the leader's superstars and overachievers to the point where they will support the leader to the fullest if they believe in the cause or oppose the leader if they do not.[60] They will risk it all if they believe in it. This can be negative to a group; a diehard will impose their views and force them on others, causing negativity, fear, and even bullying to get their way. These levels of engagement are relatable in the work environment today. Leaders must be aware of who is in their groups and what type of engagement they are giving their leaders.

There is a different lens we must look through when looking at followership. Spolin said it best, "NO, NOT LIKE THAT. IT IS ALL WRONG!"[61] She was a yeller, driven by her passion. Follow the initiator. We work hard to get to these destinations in life when all we have to do is be and follow. The following leads you to the leading, to following, to leading, to following, and to leading. I think you get the picture. Life evolves and so do our roles. We must ask ourselves as we are growing to become efficient, effective human beings. We must ask, "How do I show up? Am I an isolator with no engagement in my own world, a bystander just sitting back watching the fireworks, a participant understanding my role and the role of others, an activist willing to take a stand but slaughtering others in the process, or a diehard who causes people to cringe when I come into the room?" I can relate to each of these and have found myself having each of those behaviors at one point or another. I had to be honest about why I was there and how my behavior

60 Northouse, P. G. (2019). *Leadership: theory and practice (Eighth edition.)*. SAGE.
61 Spolin, V. (1999). *Improvisation for the theater: A handbook of teaching and directing techniques.* Northwestern University Press.

was affecting others. When you follow the FOLLOWER, you can see yourself. Sometimes it is ugly. But that is a breakthrough and the beginning of becoming.

Exercise

Meditate: Follow the FOLLOWER.

Observe: Am I the isolator, bystander, participant, activist, or the diehard?

Commit: Be honest about what I see. If it is not uplifting, change the course in my behavior.

DAY 4

*"I don't care a damn about men who are loyal
to the people who pay them."*
— **Graham Greene**

Robert Kelley stressed the importance of studying followership when it comes to leadership. Kelley sorted followers' styles from active to passive. They are broken down into five role types.[62]:

- Passive: look to the leader for direction and motivation.

- Conformist: yes-people, always on the leader's side.

- Alienated: think for themselves and have a lot of negative energy.

- Pragmatics (observers): Sit around watching and do not make any moves until they know exactly what direction the leader is going.

- Exemplary (Star): active, provides sound input, challenges decisions in a respectful way, and displays positive energy.

The star follower does not care who is paying them, who has the authority for awards and bonuses, and who gives their performance rating. They are focused on being a sounding board for the leader and organization. They have embraced the vision and goals. Star followers are there to help and remind leaders that the decisions they are making could have a negative impact and move them further from the goals. Loyalty, according to Webster's Dictionary, is the quality or state of being loyal,

---

62 Kelley, R. (1992). *The Power of Followership.* New York: Doubleday.

an allegiance.[63] Loyalty is not agreeing based on the person(s) role/position, following blindly, waiting for direction and motivation, or even staying with the group/organization. We can now make adjustments when we do not agree with or like services from an organization. We can choose to stay and fight or leave and find another place that aligns with our beliefs and expectations. Loyalty is a virtue and a part of friendship. According to Aristotle, friendship "is a virtue or implies a virtue and is besides most necessary with a view to living."[64] Aristotle believed that friendship came in two levels: high and low. The lower form is based on pleasures or utility, networking, youth, and political life. The higher form rests on genuine concern for one another and reciprocal reliance.[65] Can a person have many friends in the high form? Aristotle's position would be no, as *"it is impossible to be great friends to many."* To become friends, there must be some common ground and shared life experiences. "One must eat salt together", "become familiar with them", and "experience them"[66], which is not easily accomplished. Loyalty is not based on the characteristics of an individual but on the relationship itself.

Followership is based on relationship. If we are to believe that we can follow or lead without relationship, we have missed a key ingredient to the effectiveness of leadership. Nothing can be done without establishing relationships. We are not to manipulate people into believing that if they challenge, disagree, or provide corrective criticism, they are not loyal. Many organizations have and are suffering from misguided beliefs of what loyalty is and is not. If we want our organization to thrive, we have to be willing to allow the exemplary followers to be stars. The other follower types will see it is okay to actively think for oneself and the betterment of the organization. You do not

---

63 "loyalty." 2023. In Merriam-Webster.com. Retrieved November 14, 2023, from https://www.merriam-webster.com/dictionary/loyalty
64 Aristotle. (1155a). *Nicomachean Ethics.*
65 Fletcher, G. P. (1993). *Loyalty: an essay on the morality of relationships.* Oxford University Press.
66 Aristotle. (1155a).

have to agree as the leader, but you should provide a safe and genuine space for people to be heard and take careful consideration of what is being said.

Exercise

Meditate: Loyalty is not about agreeing with me.

Observe: Are team members coming to speak with me openly and honestly about how they feel about the direction the organization is going?

Commit: Create a space of safety and vulnerability for others to provide constructive criticism.

DAY 5

"Unchallenged behavior will dismantle organizations."
— **Reneé Murdock**

There was a man named Jess who built a beautiful family, home, and business. He had three sons, whom he raised to be upright men. When his sons were old enough to work for the business, he welcomed them gladly. The sons now had access to people's money and assets. Jess found out his sons were stealing from the people and using the business for their personal gain. He discussed the findings with his wife, and they both agreed to address the behavior. The sons acknowledged their wrong-doings, but they continued to abuse their position. The father grew weary of speaking with them but he did not remove them from the organization. Jess grew old and died, and within two years, the organization closed. The sons' unethical behavior caused the business to go into bankruptcy. The father, who was responsible for leading the organization, allowed the alienated followers (his sons) to continue in their negative and unethical behavior. He failed to remove toxic behavior for the welfare of others. The behavior did not just affect the immediate family but also the workers, communities, and families.

Leading is to follow. I wonder who Jess was following. He seems to have been an alienated follower himself. By Jess not properly addressing his sons' behaviors, a legacy of wealth was cut short. His lack of leadership and followership dismantled an economy. The behavior of leaders and followership not only affects themselves but everything they are connected to. The success of the organization depends on the followers as much as the leaders. The majority of the work and connection to the customers all go through the hands of followers.

Followers have to be independent thinkers as well as ethically sound in their decisions. Colangelo once did a study with the United States Air Force regarding those on active duty.[67] The research showed certain leadership styles affected followership styles. A democratic leadership style was related to active engagement, passion, and team collaboration. Another leadership process is called the co-created process.[68] Leading behaviors influence followers' behavior, and those behaviors have an impact on the leaders. Both the follower and the leader have an impact on one another. Leadership occurs based on the interaction with the follower and results in certain outcomes.

The characteristics of a leader are no different from those of a follower. They share the same characteristics but perform different roles. Because they share the same characteristics, the type of leader will be the same type of follower. If we use the servant leader who thinks of serving others first as an example,[69] we see that they serve followers by helping them grow personally and professionally.[70] Servant leadership effectiveness is measured by the following three questions:[71]

1. Do those whom you serve grow as persons?

2. Do they, while being served, become healthier, wiser, freer, and more autonomous?

3. Do they become servant-leaders?

Servant leaders are to produce more servants who are committed to service, trustworthy, and competent. When Jess did not clearly define the positions of the leader and the follower

67 Colangelo, A. J. (2000). *Followership: Leadership styles.* The University of Oklahoma.
68 Uhl-Bien, M., Riggio, R. E., Lowe, K. B., & Carsten, M. K. (2014, pg 83-104). *Followership theory: A review and research agenda.* The Leadership Quarterly, 25. doi: 10.1016/j.leaqua.2013.11.007.
69 Greenleaf, R. K. (1977). *Servant leadership.* Mahwah, NJ: Paulist Press.
70 Ebener, D. R., & O'Connell, D. J. (2010, pg 315-335). *How might servant leadership work?* Nonprofit Management & Leadership, 20(3), doi:10.1002/nml.256.
71 Greenleaf, R. K. (2008). *The servant as leader.* Atlanta, GA: The Greenleaf Center for Servant Leadership.

with his sons, he caused a toxic work environment. Leaders and followers have to agree on what the roles are, especially if there is another relationship outside of the professional setting.

Exercise

Meditate: Constructive criticism and conflict is not negative.

Observe: How do I respond when I am approached with conflict or questioned about my decisions?

Commit: Clearly define roles with those I have a relationship with in a personal and professional setting.

criticism.

DAY 6

"When two people always agree, one of them is unnecessary."
— **William Wrigley Jr.**

Why seek the counsel of someone who always agrees with you? If you want an honest answer, then go to the individuals who are always asking questions and do not agree with everything that is happening within the organization. A leader needs a follower who is passionate about the same things, wants the overall best for everyone, and points everything back to the goals. Cheerleaders are needed when the team is down and needs encouragement to keep going. They are also needed when you are going in the wrong direction. Have you been to a sports game where the team you are rooting for has the possession to score but they are going the wrong way? Do you hear the people on the sideline saying, "Yes, you got it. Keep going!" or do you hear, "The wrong way! You are going the wrong way!"? A good cheerleader will be able to cheer you on and warn you all at the same time.

I once read an interview about a particular CEO's approach to the leaders in the organization. The CEO said a profound thing that I had not heard or read until that day. He said, "We are raising yes-people and this is why we have yes-leaders." Wow-Wow-Wow! Think about the organizations you are a part of. Do you hear more agreement, disagreement, or curiosity? I believe we could have more people who pose questions if we allowed a place for curiosity to exist rather than treat people as though they are a threat to position, power, platforms, etc. Those who behave in this manner are led by their ego instead of a pliable heart. Who would not feel good for someone to continue to give you praise when making decisions? Principal Consultant and Founder of Business Consulting Solutions LLC, Robert Tanners, said that having an employee who agrees with you all the time makes them no longer necessary.[72] Think about it: you really don't need them as an employee or team member. You would be able to come up with ideas and carry them out. You could consult yourself for solutions. What would be the purpose of having them? You have all the answers.

Yes-people are not born. They are made. They are made out of being punished for speaking up. This can be traced back to childhood and persists into the present. When leadership shows they detest people speaking out and providing thoughts and opinions, people learn quickly to be quiet and keep their questions to themselves. Take for instance the town hall meetings senior leaders like to hold. When it comes to the "Questions and Answers" segment, the same thing happens: no one wants to say anything. The people who always talk are talking and the leaders either do not stay long, tell people to email their concerns, or become defensive. I was one of those people who would pose a question in any forum and label myself as the sacrificial lamb. Some colleagues were okay with me taking this role for the team because the culture that was created was that if you speak out, you are marked as rebellious, disrespectful, disloyal, self-serving, or out to get their position. Sadly, I have to say this was not one but many organizations I have been a part of. This goes to show there is a lot to be done by us as human beings, as leaders, and as followers in terms of the environment we create for others.

Mr. William Wrigley was a great industrialist and business-man. He believed in creating jobs for communities and helping those in need. He looked to others for insight and their opinions when doing business. Mr. Wrigley was not in the business of having teams to follow his every move. He wanted honest feed-

---

72 Tanner R, (2021). *The danger of creating yes people.* https://managementisajourney.com/the-danger-of-creating-yes-people/

back on the direction the organization was going.[73] To get the best result is to allow people to have their own creative voice. You are not giving them a voice; they already have one. You are giving them a safe space to say what they think and say it LOUD!

Exercise

Meditate: A one-man team will never accomplish all it was set out to do.

Observe: Do people speak out in meetings? How do I respond to their comments?

Commit: Become more curious and take into consideration others' opinions.

---

73 Tanner R, (2021). *The danger of creating yes people.* https://managementisajourney.com/the-danger-of-creating-yes-people/

DAY 7

Today is the day to reflect on the past six days. Review what we've already learned or answer the following questions:

- Do you see yourself as both a follower and a leader?

- What type of follower are you?

- Are you able to see yourself having been all types at one point in your life? What was going on at the time? Are you able to pinpoint the type of environment you were working in?

- How do you view loyalty? Are you a loyal person?

- Are you able to take constructive criticism?

Followership and leadership are the same. You cannot have leadership without followership. To become a great leader, you must first become a great follower. Too many people want to be at the top and forget something must be at the bottom holding it up. *Effective followers* are those who work alongside the leader, pushing, driving, and challenging the development of ideas and decision-making. They keep the goals of the organization at the forefront when posing questions and concerns. They get the job done. They learn from their leaders and support them.[74] They are not yes-people. They are not people who sit by the wayside waiting to be told what to do. They are the game changers.

Lipman-Blumen posed a question: Why do people follow bad leaders? She identified six psychological factors that followers fall into when it comes to helping destructive and/or toxic leaders. She states that there is a need for security and certainty, to

---

74 Lapierre, L. M., & Carstein, M. K. (Eds.) (2014). *Followership: what is it and why do people follow? (First edition.).* Emerald.

feel chosen or special, a need for in the human community, fear of ostracism, isolation, and social death, and fear of powerlessness to challenge a bad leader.[75]

Visit https://edge.sagepub.com/northouse8e to take the Followership questionnaire. The questionnaire is a tool to help you determine what type of follower you are from an empirical approach.[76]

75 Lipman-Blumen, J. (2005). *The allure of toxic leaders.* Oxford University Press.
76 Northouse, P. G. (2019). *Leadership: theory and practice (Eighth edition.).* SAGE.

References

Aretha Sills with Carol Sills. (2023, November 17). Retrieved from https://www.violaspolin.org/bio

Aristotle. (n.d.). Nicomachean Ethics (1155a).

Bligh, M. C. (2011). Followership and follower-centred approaches. In A. Bryman, K. Grint, B. Jackson, M. Uhl-Bien, & D. Collinson (Eds.), *The Sage handbook of leadership* (pp. 1180-1216). Sage.

Chaleff, I. (2008). Creating new ways of following. In R. Riggio, I. Chaleff, & J. Lipman-Blumen (Eds.), *The art of followership: How great followers create great leaders and organizations* (pp. 67–87). San Francisco: Jossey-Bass.

Colangelo, A. J. (2000). Followership: Leadership styles. The University of Oklahoma.

Crossman, B., & Crossman, J. (2011). Conceptualising followership – a review of the literature. *Leadership*, 7(4), 481–497. doi:10.1177/1742715011416891

Crowther, S. (2018). *Biblical servant leadership: An exploration of leadership for the contemporary context.* Springer International Publishing.

Davis, C. J. (Ed.). (2017). *Servant leadership and followership: Examining the impact on workplace behavior* (1st ed.). Springer International Publishing. https://doi.org/10.1007/978-3-319-59366-1

Ebener, D. R., & O'Connell, D. J. (2010). How might servant leadership work? *Nonprofit Management & Leadership*, 20(3), 315–335. doi:10.1002/nml.256

Fletcher, G. P. (1993). *Loyalty: An essay on the morality of relationships.* Oxford University Press.

Follower. (2023). In *Merriam-Webster.com*. Retrieved November 14, 2023, from https://www.merriam-webster.com/dictionary/follower

Gaunt, D. (2022). Ego and authority. In *Ego, authority, failure*. BookBaby.

Greenleaf, R. K. (1977). *Servant leadership*. Mahwah, NJ: Paulist Press.

Greenleaf, R. K. (2008). *The servant as leader*. Atlanta, GA: The Greenleaf Center for Servant Leadership.

Kellerman, B. (2008). *Followership: How followers are creating change and changing leaders*. Boston, MA: Harvard Business School Publishing.

Kelley, R. (1988). In praise of followers. *Harvard Business Review*, 66(6), 142–148.

Kelley, R. (1992). *The power of followership*. New York: Doubleday.

Lapierre, L. M., & Carsten, M. K. (Eds.). (2014). *Followership: What is it and why do people follow?* (1st ed.). Emerald.

Lipman-Blumen, J. (2005). *The allure of toxic leaders*. Oxford University Press.

Loyalty. (2023). In *Merriam-Webster.com*. Retrieved November 14, 2023, from https://www.merriam-webster.com/dictionary/loyalty

Northouse, P. G. (2019). *Leadership: Theory and practice* (8th ed.). Sage.

Patterson, K. A. (2003). Servant leadership: A theoretical model. Paper presented at the Servant Leadership Roundtable.

Riggio, R. E., Chaleff, I., & Lipman-Blumen, J. (Eds.). (2008). *The art of followership: How great followers create great leaders and organizations* (1st ed.). Jossey-Bass.

Robinson, D. (2004). Marketing gum, making meanings: Wrigley in North America, 1890–1930. *Enterprise & Society*, 5(1), 4–44.

Spolin, V. (1999). *Improvisation for the theater: A handbook of teaching and directing techniques.* Northwestern University Press.

Tanner, R. (2021). The danger of creating yes people. Retrieved from https://managementisajourney.com/the-danger-of-creating-yes-people/

Uhl-Bien, M., Riggio, R. E., Lowe, K. B., & Carsten, M. K. (2014). Followership theory: A review and research agenda. *The Leadership Quarterly*, 25, 83–104. doi:10.1016/j.leaqua.2013.11.007

Zaleznik, A. (1965). The dynamics of subordinacy. *Harvard Business Review*, 43(3), 119–131.

PART 5

HEARTSTRINGS AND HANDSHAKES

How do we know if we are maturing in our leadership roles? Let's talk about our relationships. Webster defines *relation* as how two or more concepts, objects, or people are connected or the state of being connected.[77] The key here is coming together. There is only a connection if there is a coming together. Leaders have to come together with followers not just in a professional way but also on a personal level. Do not count out this methodology just yet. I know you have been taught to separate the two; do not mix and mingle. Leave home at home and leave work at work. Ask yourself if this is genuinely realistic. We spend most of our waking hours with the people we work with, not our family. We put things in place to connect with family but with a different emphasis on work. The Hebrew word for relationship is מערכת יחסים, which means link, tie, knot, proximity, attitude, treatment, proportion, friendship, and kinship. Also, it links to love or ***ahava,*** which is made up of three basic Hebrew letters: aleph (א), hey (ה), and vet (ב). We get the root word, hav, which means to give.[78]

Relationships are seen as less valuable in the workplace. Western culture has taught us that they are seen as transactional and beneficial of what one can gain from another individual. We look for individual ways to solve problems. When Asian culture sees a problem, they evaluate their relationships. Problems with employee engagement, empowerment, organizational agility, and innovation can all be solved by taking action in our relationships and by becoming more personalized and collaborative.[79] As long as leader-follower relationships remain impersonal, the deception, high turnover rates, and power abuse will remain unresolved.

77 "relation." 2023. In Merriam-Webster.com. Retrieved November 20, 2023, from https://www.merriam-webster.com/dictionary/relation

78 Strong, J., Kohlenberger, J. R., Swanson, J. A., & Strong, J. (2001). *The strongest Strong's exhaustive concordance of the Bible* (Twenty-first century edition, fully revised and corrected by John R. Kohlenberger III and James A. Swanson.). Zondervan.

79 Schein, E. H., & Schein, P. A. (2018). *Humble leadership: the powers of relationships, openness, and trust.* Berrett-Koehler.

When it comes to the way we interact with each other, organizations operate in a hierarchical, bureaucratic way. Leadership development is like gold mining. You will not find it overnight; there are layers. You must get through long hours, hard physical labor, uncomfortable positions, and technical training. Our world has suffered dramatically because of the lack of healthy relationships. Families have been torn apart by divorce, parents torn from children, children torn from parents, supervisors at odds with employees, landlords at odds with tenants, and religious communities at odds with one another.

There have been years of research on how organizations should be structured in terms of leadership roles. How we work has gotten complex and is still changing. Schein suggests we need to change the leadership model to *Humble Leadership* based on these factors:

1. **Task complexity is increasing**. Technology and geographical social networks have created new ways to communicate and work, making it harder to define the leadership process.

2. **The current managerial culture is myopic, has blind spots, and is often self-defeating**. Often, the problems are not with individuals but with the interaction of relationships. There is mistrust both upwards and downwards in the hierarchy.

3. **There are generational changes in social and work values**. The generation that has recently entered the workforce is looking for meaningful work, ways to fulfill their talents, and the opportunity to gain experience. They are not looking for bonuses and wealthy salaries.[80]

Humble Leadership is leadership that is built on trust and openness. There are different levels of relationships, and some argue that the closeness of a leader with followers causes more issues. I once led a group in an organization, and one person

---

80 Schein, E. H., & Schein, P. A. (2018). *Humble leadership: the powers of relationships, openness, and trust.* Berrett-Koehler.

on the team went to the same place of worship as I did. At the place of worship, the person would refer to me in the same way as in the other work organization. One day, I pulled them aside and told them it was okay to call me by my first name and not my title. We could interact with one another just as we would with other congregation members. We did not have issues in either organization, and the relationship at work was stronger. The relationship allowed me to connect with the other team members meaningfully.

The connection does not mean opening up my bedroom and inviting everyone in. There can be proximity and connectivity. One example is the relationship you have with your primary doctor. There is a level of trust and openness automatically, and as time goes on, you become more comfortable telling them more intimate information. The caution to *Humble Leadership* is the ability to manage this balance between being too formal at one extreme and being too intimate at the other extreme.[81]

There are problems not just with leadership, but also with our relationships. If we do great work together, then we must connect. Connections can be found in many ways; leaders and followers must be willing to be open to those connections. The connection between two human beings is more important than other factors.[82] Kouzes and Posner, in their book *The Leadership Challenge*, argue that leaders' success depends "upon the capacity to build and sustain those human relationships that enable people to get extraordinary things done regularly." What matters most is the relationship between the leader and follower to get effective results.[83]

81 Schein, E. H., & Schein, P. A. (2018)

82 Heifetz, R. & Linsky, M. (2002, pg 75). *Leadership on the line: staying alive through the dangers of leading.* Harvard Business Press Review.

83 Kouzes, J.M., Posner, B.Z. (2008, pg 24-25). *The Leadership Challenge.* Jossey-Bass.

DAY 1

"What draws people to be friends is that they see the same truth. They share it."
— C.S. Lewis

We often take the word "friend" too lightly. For a child in school aged 4 to 8, everyone is their friend. As they get older, the friend list becomes shorter, and there are more changes in who their friends are. We have more acquaintances than friends. A friend is someone you know; there is a mutual bond of affection and exclusivity. There is no hostility, and they are not your enemy. The term "acquaintances" was used to mean "friend" just before the 19th century as someone close, but it has since turned into someone who nods. This is someone with whom there is no proximity, no knowledge of who they are; when you see them, there is a nod or a kind acknowledgment of their presence. The word "friend" originated from Frēond, the Old English verb frēon, which meant "to love, like, honor, set free (from slavery or confinement); from the Germanic ancestor of Old English originally meant "one who loves." We can see that having a friend is having a bond of mutual affection, loving them, and not harming them. The self-gratification of human nature keeps us from true friendship through fear, lack of commitment, pride, ego, and selfishness.

Relationships take work; if I want to have a friendship, I must be willing to do some work. Most of us are lazy when it comes to relationships, which is why marriages end in divorce. We stopped being friends and are now becoming acquaintances or even enemies, allowing the connection to die. When we are fond of someone and are pursuing their attention, work goes into it. You take time to learn about them, put what you learn into action, and make sure there is time to learn more. There are countless hours of talking, texting, chatting, etc., to form a mutual bond of affection. Both parties did not mutually agree on affection or attraction from the beginning. There is a gentleman named Jamie Kilstein, and he is talking about his dating life (so comical). He says, "I am not a good-looking guy, so I have to get the lady with my personality and my humor and show her I am seriously interested. I do not have the smooth pickup lines, the Roman god's body, or even the Dolce Gabbana clothing. So, you dudes who are just trying to smack it, cut it out, so us regular guys who want an honest relationship can have a chance, rather than the girl smacking you because you told her, her hairstyle is nice." The point is that there are people who want honest, grounded, effective relationships and are not looking for self-fulfillment; they are willing to put in the work. All relationships require work, whether they are personal or professional.

Why is it that I cannot have a friend at work? Why is it not allowed to have a team member or employee as a friend? Relationships are often seen as purely transactional in the bureaucratic and hierarchical structure. We communicate from a place of legitimate power based on position. The way leaders use their power has shifted to followers.[84] Followers come from a position of information power. They have the information and skills the leaders need to meet their goals. This is why negative conflict and power struggles occur. Although both types of power are needed, how they are being used affects the connection. In a relationship, the power is mutual and is shared for the benefit of a shared outcome. Friendships are achievable with team members and employees. If we change our mindsets from dominion to connectivity, from "follow me" to a leader-follower

84 Kellerman, B. (2019). *The Future Of Followership. Strategy & Leadership*, 47(5), 42-46. doi:10.1108/SL-07-2019-0109

exchange, from "I have the answers" to "I am learning something new," we could build friendships with healthy boundaries.

Who enjoys war? I know I am not a fan. So, why do leaders create hostile work environments with those we should be in community with and have mutual affection for? Leaders must find ways to be at peace with one another. You have to work for it. Peace has to be in our hearts as something to work toward. What is in the heart, man will do. I encourage you to work toward the truth of meaningful relationships in the workplace. Leave behind the old way of thinking of "What can they do for me?" and put on the new mentality of "What can we do together?"

Exercise

Meditate: Relationship and friendship takes intentional work.

Observe: Do I only reach out to my team members when I need something? Do I genuinely care about their well-being and growth?

Commit: Evaluate my relationships. Be intentional about building time in my day to build effective friendships.

DAY 2

"Every person in this life has something to teach me -- and as soon as I accept that, I open myself to truly listening."
— **Catherine Doucette**

Remaining teachable and being a lifelong learner provokes transformation in one's soul. Can you read an article, quote, sign, book, or even caption without thinking about the who, what, when, and why? Leading requires deep thinking. Encountering others should cause a person to become curious. When we become curious, there is a genuine thought of concern about the other person. Showing interest in what someone is doing, saying, or feeling is a tool for building a relationship.

I want to shift gears a bit and talk about the cartoon *"Curious George (CG)."* (I am not a fan. I could not understand CG's inability to talk and the commentator's voice.) It was a good series, even though it was not my go-to cartoon—Alvin & the Chipmunks! Before the cartoon, it was a book series by a Jewish couple (Hans Augusto (H. A.) Rey and Margret Rey) who fled from Paris in 1940. CG was captured in Africa by "the man with the big yellow hat' and placed in a zoo in America. CG escapes, and the man finds him and takes him home to live with him. CG frequently gets into challenging situations due to his curiosity, and the man always helps him out. In every episode I've encountered the man becomes curious due to George's inquisitiveness. What's remarkable about their relationship is they grow together. Even though he is educated, employed, a world traveler, he continues to learn from George. I strongly disagree with the saying, *"You cannot teach an old dog a new trick."* If they are willing, they can learn something new.

A leader's performance and success point to how they view relationships. If you want to get extraordinary things done, sustaining human relationships should matter first.[85] There are two perspectives in a relationship: individual and relational. Currently, our organizations need help with the blame game. Why do you think this is? For the most part, we think of things individually instead of collectively. An individual perspective focuses on who made what decision along the way and puts the blame on the person they believe was the driving force. From a collective perspective, the team is moving together, and when something goes wrong, each person looks at themselves to see what they could have done better.[86]

From an individual perspective, the leader relationships become weaker due to their narrow outlook. They believe that there's only one way and only one person can be right; people either get it or they do not.[87] Recently, my hubby and I went to an event for married couples. There was an exercise we had to do listing the weaknesses and strengths of our marriage. My love wrote "communication" in both areas. I disagreed, and we spent most of the time discussing our positions. During the briefing, other couples agreed there could be an argument for both sides. My love wanted me to switch my viewpoint, so I agreed to disagree with him. The point is that because of our mutual connection and wanting the best for each other, there was no reason to fall out because of different viewpoints. There is too much time spent on small matters in the workplace. If you don't like how they addressed you in a meeting, instead of getting upset, approach them with curiosity. I guarantee that the issue is not you. We are often too easily offended. From a relational perspective, one thing is on everyone's mind: rela-

---

85 Kouzes, J.M., Posner, B.Z. (2008, pg 24-25). *The Leadership Challenge*. Jossey-Bass.
86 Smith, D. M. (2011). *Elephant in the room : how relationships make or break the success of leaders and organizations (1st ed.)*. Jossey-Bass.
87 Smith, D. M. (2011).

tionship, then mission. If the relationship is not working, the mission will not work.

Take, for instance, Steve Jobs and John Sculley. The relationship was horrible, and Apple suffered and probably would not exist today if Sculley not put his ego aside. Roosevelt and Churchill had different views on many things, but they were willing to take the time to listen to one another's views.[88] When Roosevelt was attacked publicly by the British Parliament for not wanting to join the war, Churchill came to his defense, even though he had been hesitant about joining it in the past. Churchill was able to defend Roosevelt because he had taken the time to listen to his views on the war and other political topics. He did not agree with him on everything, but he understood him. Churchill's last words to Roosevelt before he died were, "Amantium irae amoris integratio est" (Latin), translation: "Lovers' quarrels always go with true love." [89]

Disagreements, challenges, pressure, failures, and mistakes will happen. How you handle them is a choice. Will you look through the lens of an individual or a relational perspective? While it may be easy to say, it will be challenging to do until relationships are the focal point.

Exercise

Meditate: Curiosity creates learning.

Observe: How do I listen to others? What new things do I learn daily and from whom?

Commit: Keep a lens of relational perspective. When I disagree with others, ask more questions to learn and understand them.

---

88 NPS. (November, 2015). *Roosevelt and Churchill: A friendship that saved the world.* https://www.nps.gov/articles/fdrww2.htm
89 Meacham, J. (2003). *Franklin and Winston: An intimate portrait of an epic friendship.* Random House

DAY 3

The ocean is a massive body of saltwater. Oceanographers have broken it down into four distinct sections: Arctic, Atlantic, Indian, and Pacific, but it is essentially one giant ocean. The ocean covers about 71% of the Earth's surface. 97% of the water we use comes from the ocean. Some parts of the ocean are so deep you would not see the top of Mount Everest if placed there. The average depth is 12,200 feet. Only 20% of the ocean has been explored by humans, which means there is still 80% that still needs to be discovered.[90] Space has been explored more than the ocean. Okay, this is not a geography course—we can learn much about workplace relationships from just a tiny portion of the information shared here.

One drop of water cannot make a massive body of water. I believe we are like the ocean. Only 20% of it has been discovered because the necessary equipment is needed to get to the other parts. Our products or services have not reached certain parts of the Earth because we need the resources. The top five companies in the world in 2023 are Apple, Microsoft, Saudi Aramco, Alphabet (Google), and Amazon, which are worth $2.7 to 1.4 trillion dollars. These companies have pushed society into technological innovation through products, software, oil and gas, hardware, and e-commerce. I am not saying they are the only ones who got it right. They understand and value relationships and working in teams instead of being the lone

---

90 Boudreau et. al, October 2019. *All about the Ocean.* https://www.nationalgeographic.com/environment/topic/oceans

ranger. We have yet to scratch the surface of achieving great things on the Earth based on our abilities to come together. When individuals come together, they will have a more extensive reach. Some areas need products and services to improve communities. The depth of what human beings are capable of is limitless. However, our limitless abilities do have their limits. But you just said "limitless!" Yes, we are limitless within the constructs of our talents and limited to global impact. Our limitation is set on what should be all things to all people.

There was a show in the 90s called "In Living Color." It was a sketch comedy show that aired on Fox Channel for four years. The show helped many comedians make it into mainstream filming. The show gained international prominence and won a Primetime Emmy Award. There was a skit on the show called "Hey Mon" about a Jamaican family with many jobs and other businesses. In those businesses, one family member is the bellhop, receptionist, host, and maintenance worker. The skits are hilarious; you should go check them out. The family showed that no matter how many jobs they had, they never got ahead because they needed to allow those who did it well to be excellent in what they did. Leaders must be willing to share in the organization's mission and vision. Everyone has a role in life, family, and workplace. No actual traction occurs when we walk out, are pushed out, or wait it out.

The way we work and communicate has changed drastically. Teams now meet virtually 95% of their workweek. We come together through email, phone, video chats, instant messaging, and social media. Even with all of those different ways, there is still a disconnect between team members and supervisors. We need to change how we think and how we come together. The younger generation is looking for significance, belonging, two-way contribution, and personal and professional fulfillment.[91] Those who have been in the workforce for some time have

91 Silver, S. R., & Franz, T. M. (2021). *Meaningful partnership at work : how the workplace covenant ensures mutual accountability and success between leaders and teams.* Productivity Press. https://doi.org/10.4324/9781003181477

LEADERSHIP EVOLUTION

worked in the frame of shallow and exploitative relationships. An effective leader desires to reach as many people as they can. How they go about it is what hinders the organization from advancing. I am not an expert in emotional wounds, but they play a significant role in how we show up and behave toward others. I challenge you to read some literature on emotional wounds; if you have not been to counseling, it will provoke you to enroll. Silver and Franz say that without empathy, respect, trust, alignment, and partnership (ERTAP), there will not be a connection.[92] Coming together is a beginning; keeping together is progress; working together is success.[93]

Exercise

Meditate: I am a small piece of the bigger picture.

Observe: How do team members respond to each other? What strengths and weaknesses do I see in each team member?

Commit: Re-evaluate my team's needs every quarter and listen to them in word and deed.

---

92 Silver, S. R., & Franz, T. M. (2021). *Meaningful partnership at work : how the workplace covenant ensures mutual accountability and success between leaders and teams.* Productivity Press. https://doi.org/10.4324/9781003181477
93 Ford, H. (2012). *Coming together is a beginning. Keeping together is a process. Working together is success.*

DAY 4

*"One man can be a crucial ingredient on a team,
but one man cannot make a team."*
— **Kareem Abdul-Jabbar**

Let's talk about basketball. A basketball court measures 91.86 feet long and 49.21 feet wide. There are sidelines, baselines, end lines, mid-court, center circle, three-point line, free throw line, free throw circle, backboards, and the basketball goal, each having specified dimensions to be in regulations. A team consists of ten players, five from each side, who run up and down the court to get one orange ball into the goal. The teams are allowed to have 12 players on the roster, but only five can play from each side while the ball is in play. One National Basketball Association (NBA) game consists of a 12-minute quarter with four quarters totaling 48 minutes, where players try to get as many points as possible to win. The team has to know the rules and possess specific skills to play: dribbling, shooting, line of sight, forward-thinking, rebounding, defending, passing, speed, endurance, acrobatic ability, and agility. Each skill can be done individually but must be used collectively. One person cannot get the most points if there is not another person to pass them the ball, defend their opponent, rebound the misses, and push them to keep going. Many teams within the NBA lineup have won the National Championship; two teams throughout 74 championships have taken 34 in total. The Lakers and Celtics are tied as of 2023 with 17 championships apiece. There are eleven teams out of 30 who have never won a title. The Celtics are the only team in the history of the NBA to have won eight consecutive championships from 1959-1966. How were they able to do it?

One person's skills are insufficient to get the most significant return. Do you think that all twelve players were on the court, playing at the same time? Everyone on the team played a role on and off the court. For the team concept to work, there must be respect for what each member has to bring, psychological safety where there is no negativity in judging others' views and opinions, the value of everyone's contributions, support and encouragement for one another, transparency when making decisions, taking ownership of mistakes, and always keeping one thing at the forefront—why we are here? Conflict will arise; it is how we handle the conflicts that matters.

In 1989, Kimberlé Crenshaw conducted a study of inter-sections between different disenfranchised or marginalized groups.[94] The study begins by recognizing that individuals experience multiple intersecting identities that flow from different life experiences. The overlapping stems are determined by culture, race, class, gender, and sexual orientation. The Intersectionality Methodology is designed to help deconstruct conflict, bring the conflict narrative to light, and revise the framework of conflict engagement.[95]

When emotions are high, we sometimes need to acknowledge the person(s) emotions. There is no getting around them. There is a space between our present world and the one we desire. Emotions can bring us into a realization of this gap.[96] A healthy form of continuous dialogue seeking to understand people's views is evident in academia, where the space for conflict is constructively embraced. Outside these structures, the idea of one seeking out understanding is a waste of time, and someone has to win. There is a power struggle of who will dominate the other. Leaders are to encourage emotions, destabilize myths about

94 Crenshaw, K. (1991). *Mapping the Margins: Intersectionality, Identity Politics, and Violence against Women of Color.* Stanford Law Review 43, no. 6, 1241 1299.
95 Kellett, P. M., & Matyok, T. G. (Eds.) (2016). *Transforming conflict through communication in personal, family, and working relationships.* Lexington Books.
96 Ahmed, S. (2004). *The Cultural Politics of Emotion.* Routledge

emotions, and aim toward creative discomfort. Teams will learn to respect and value each other's views. Everyone is a winner.

Bill Russell, an NBA National Hall of Fame inductee, was the winner of 11 national championships in his 13-year career. He was not the best player; he was the second overall pick by the St. Louis Hawks. He was traded to the Boston Celtics for Ed Macauley, Cliff Hagan, and the Celtics' seventh overall pick (Auerbach knew precisely what he was doing). The Hawks won the championship in 1958 until Bill got grounded in his role. Everything Bill did was for the good of the team. He was not the number one shooting guard or above-the-rim trailblazer. Bill would shut down the opponent to provide opportunities for the team to capitalize on. He was fascinating. You knew his passion by what he said. He questioned just about everything and had an opinion on everything. Why were the Celtics able to win eight consecutive titles? Because one man showed up and modeled the art of teamwork to which those around him got on board. When a first round draft pick is chosen, this does not equate to immediate success. While individual talent is valuable, its often the collective effort and synergy of a team that leads to victory. Whether in sports, business, or any endeavor, working together can unlock greater potential.

Exercise

Meditate: All skills are valuable for everyone.

Observe: Look at the team I am leading or a specific member. How does each person show up? How do they respond to one another? How do they acknowledge one another's emotions?

Commit: Embrace conflict and create a space for healthy conflict where people become uncomfortable.

DAY 5

"If you want to lift yourself up, lift up someone else."
— **Booker T. Washington**

Booker T. Washington's words may be hard to swallow. Society tells us to go out and get it, climb high, do not let anyone stop you, strive to be the best, etc. Steve Harvey a television personality, shares that many people are hesitant to take risk, which prevents them discovering their purpose. Continuously seeking and having deep faith are essential for finding that purpose. The purpose in life is connecting and serving others. We are here to serve others. We are here on Earth to connect with others. Have you ever been in the store and someone did not have enough money at the register and you helped pay? Or you saw a person on the corner asking for food or money and you helped? Or someone needed a ride to and from work and you helped? In those moments, you walked away with a feeling of "I am glad I was able to help." There is a warm, genuine, grateful feeling that you were in a position to help. In those moments, you may feel uplifted, accomplished, and valued. Mr. Washington is pointing out that we should always take this stance.

Leaders spend too much time on their ambitions while neglecting their teams. Do not get me wrong; I am not saying not to grow (I mean, you would not be reading this book if you did not believe in growth). I am saying you can grow and learn while building others up. Governor John Winthrop gave a speech in 1630 reminding the leaders, "We are like a city that sits on a hill for all people to see." Governor Winthrop had a religious approach to leading, but other officials throughout the centuries have used this same approach. The actual saying is in Matthew 5:14.[97] Jesus is giving a speech to a crowd about how their attitude in life should be and who they are on Earth—a light that cannot be hidden. A light gives exposure to areas that were not easily seen before. Leaders ought to be like light, shining for others to see the path that was invisible before. Living a life of high morals is what it will take to lead and build value-based relationships.[98]

We teach one another in the workplace from a place of hierarchy, rule-based, and loyalty where trust is lacking and morality has no true value. A study from 1932 to 1972 called "Tuskegee Syphilis" was conducted by the U.S. Public Health Services. The participants were 600 African American males.399 had syphilis and 201 did not have the disease. The men were told they were being treated for bad blood, and if they took part, they would get free medical exams, free meals, and free burial insurance.[99] Nearly ten years later, in 1943, penicillin was used to treat syphilis, but the men in the study did not receive treatment until 1973. The study was published in 1972, an ad hoc medical panel was convened to terminate the study in treating all remaining participants, their wives, and children.[100] Hannah Arendt called this type of situation the "banality of evil", and it was not limited to the Nazis.[101] [102] I encourage you to look up the whole study to see how leaders can lose sight of their purpose. Who would commit such a cruel act when there were means for medical treatment? The answer is leaders who do not value relationships, who do not value the lives of others, and who do not value themselves.

---

97 English Standard Version Bible. (2020). ESV online. www.biblegateway.com

98 Newell, T., Reeher, G., & Ronayne, P. (2012). *The Trusted Leader: Building the Relationships that Make Government Work (Second edition)*. CQ Press. https://doi.org/10.4135/9781506335667

99 Vonderlehr, R.A., Clark, T., Wenger, O.C., Heller, J.R. (1936). *Untreated Syphilis in the Male Negro*. Journal of Venereal Disease Information.

100 "HEW News" Office of the Secretary. (March 1973). *USPHS Study of Untreated Syphilis (the Tuskegee Study; Authority to Treat Participants Upon Termination of the Study*." Memorandum from Wilmot R Hastings to the secretary.

101 Newell, T., Reeher, G., & Ronayne, P. (2012).

102 Arendt. (1963).

There are similar immoralities happening today in organizations, and there needs to be someone who can change the course of history; what we are taught, whether verbal or modeling, will continue to be passed down from generation to generation. Why not teach the next leaders how to put others first, hold the ladder for others to climb, and help others in their growth that will benefit everyone? An attitude of servitude is not just for the holidays or special occasions; every day, you should strive to lift others to better your organizations, communities, families, and yourself.

Exercise

Meditate: I am a city that sits on a hill for all to see.

Observe: Who am I lifting up each day? Am I aware of any unethical issues that I have not addressed?

Commit: Lift up others who are willing to be lifted.

DAY 6

"The deeper your relationship with others, the more effective your leadership will be. People will not follow you if they do not trust you, and before someone will lend you a hand, you must first touch their heart."
— **Robin Sharma**

There is a show on Netflix called "Young Sheldon." Although it is fictional, it was inspired by one of the writers of "Big Bang Theory." Young Sheldon does not like to touch hands; when it is time for dinner prayer, he puts on mittens. One day, his dad tells him that it is not pleasant to go around telling people about all the wrong others are doing; it can cause him more harm than good. He tells Sheldon they moved because he told on a bunch of people at work, and he was the one fired. At dinner that night, during prayer, Young Sheldon removed his left-hand mitt to touch his father's hand (this was the first time he touched his father's hand), and they exchanged a beautiful smile.[103] Sheldon's dad touched his heart; this was an unusual feeling Sheldon was experiencing. His father was vulnerable in telling his story. He admired his dad for sharing and wanted to show him the bravery of opening up. Relationships take bravery, whether they are personal or professional. To have a relationship is to become vulnerable to others. The thing about vulnerability is that there is no guarantee that others will receive or value it.

We have lost social connection in the information era due to technology. I am pro-technology, but there is a cost we are paying without healthy boundaries. The average person spends

---

103 Chuck Lorre, Bill Prady, Steve Molaro, Todd Spiewak. (2017). *Young Sheldon.* Watch Young Sheldon | Netflix.

a quarter of their day wrapped around it. Unless you buy a subscription, those ads that keep popping up (so annoying) are there to make shareholders more money. Social media platforms are marketed as tools to connect, but we are more disconnected than ever. Individuals are experiencing, anxiety, and depression, not being able to connect, or being bullied. They are pressured into specific behaviors. People will text first before calling. They will watch shorts and take them as factual; next thing you know, they are marching down the street with picket signs. The goal is to get at least 1,000 followers to start; anything below and you are considered irrelevant. Erwin says, "We might be able to communicate with everyone, but it is difficult to get close to anyone."[104] The pandemic did not help in the matter of connectivity; it amplified the challenge. People figured out they could work effectively, spend time with their family, and not sit in traffic for hours, have to drive back and forth for health appointments, miss children's activities, leave the house when it is dark, and return when it is dark. No one wants to spend 40 hours working and taking time away from their loved ones.

The more time you spend with someone, the deeper the connection. All is not lost in connecting with others in a virtual space. Creativity and intentionality are key.[105] How often have you checked your device while someone is speaking to you? How many times have you been in a meeting and spent the time answering emails, writing emails, or sending IMs and text messages? We have convinced ourselves that we can multitask and still be effective. Cliff Nass, a psychology professor at Stanford University, studied the effects of multitasking. He discovered that those who do multiple things simultaneously need to be more focused on one particular area. They have trained their brain to become fleeting as they continue to function in this manner. The brain is not elastic; it does not just snap back

104 Erwin, M. S., & DeVoll, W. (2022). *Leadership is a relationship: how to put people first in the digital world.* John Wiley & Sons, Inc.
105 Erwin, M. S., & DeVoll, W. (2022).

into shape. Multitasking is a waste of time and has killed people's concentration and creativity.[106]

I never realized how much of a distraction a "multitasker" could be until a person joined the team I was on. In every meeting, I'm not joking—this person checked their smartphone or watch at least five times and sent messages in between. I just continued with the meeting, but it affected the team because a few people started to complain. The person only stayed on the team for a short time. The lack of connection was evident from all parties; if it wasn't, there would have been more curiosity instead of complaining and blaming.

There is a human desire in all of us to connect in meaningful ways. The way we work is not "going back" to how it used to be. How we currently work is less effective in building necessary relationships. The expectation of being "on" all the time is not realistic. There is so much noise around and deliverables are piling up or are never-ending. Who is taking the time to be human? When I look back on the leaders with whom I had an excellent relationship, I would be there for them day or night. They were human, not superficial superhumans. They had families and shortcomings, and I admired them for all of it. I would talk, and I knew they were listening because there was action behind those words of encouragement, guidance, praise, and correction. If you are going to become an effective leader, you must put *PEOPLE FIRST*. I can guarantee the work will get done if you are okay with your humanity.

Exercise

Meditate: Leadership is relational.

Observe: How am I vulnerable?

Commit: Focus on one thing at a time. Place boundaries on my social media interaction. Be present with others.

---

106 Flatow, I., "*The Myth of Multitasking*," NPR, May 10, 2013, https://www.npr.org/2013/05/10/182861382/the-myth-of-multitasking.

DAY 7

Take the time today to reflect on the past six days of learning.

- Are you friends with your employees or teammates?

- How have you been vulnerable with them?

- Do you listen to others in your area of work? If so, what were the results?

- What individuals are you lifting up? Make a list.

- What have you learned from others this week? Did you tell them it was new to you?

- Do you pass the ball, or are you always taking the shot?

Relationships take work and can be complex. In all the complexity, there are great rewards in building meaningful connections. One person cannot do it all; things are liable to fall through or you'll become burned out. Social connection is in every being on Earth: Deoxyribonucleic Acid (DNA). There is a twisting and winding of how we are all connecting, and when the connection is not there, it feels like the parting of the Red Sea. How we communicate, behave, as well as our maturity level, ethnicity, gender, sexual orientation, and class all affect how we connect. Individuals have to be sensitive to their own biases in how they approach building relationships. Are you quick to build with someone who looks like you, talks like you, or comes from the same background as you? If we are honest with ourselves, we tend to flock to those things that are familiar because we do not like to be uncomfortable.

Get it through your head right now: comfort is a hindrance to your development. Having diverse surroundings opens up your mindset to new ideas. Vulnerability saves you from yourself, shame, and the opinions of others. All humans want to do something, and we need a nudge or two, five or even hundreds, to get us there. The person willing to do the nudging through vulnerability, accountability, motivation, persuasion, and creativity is leading. The position or title does not make the leader. Do you want to lead and lead well? Then, keep people first.

References

Ahmed, S. (2004). *The cultural politics of emotion*. Routledge.

Archer, D., & Cameron, A. (2013). *Collaborative leadership: Building relationships, handling conflict and sharing control* (2nd ed.). Routledge. https://doi.org/10.4324/9780203067505

Arendt, H. (1963).

Boudreau, B., et al. (2019, October). All about the ocean. National Geographic. https://www.nationalgeographic.com/environment/topic/oceans

Crenshaw, K. (1991). Mapping the margins: Intersectionality, identity politics, and violence against women of color. *Stanford Law Review, 43*(6), 1241–1299.

Drucker, P. F. (2011). *The essential Drucker: Selections from the management works of Peter F. Drucker* (Classic Drucker collection ed., rev. ed.). Routledge.

English Standard Version Bible. (2020). *Bible Gateway*. ESV Online. www.biblegateway.com

Erwin, M. S., & DeVoll, W. (2022). *Leadership is a relationship: How to put people first in the digital world*. John Wiley & Sons, Inc.

Flatow, I. (2013). The myth of multitasking. NPR. https://www.npr.org/2013/05/10/182861382/the-myth-of-multitasking

Heifetz, R., & Linsky, M. (2002). *Leadership on the line: Staying alive through the dangers of leading* (p. 75). Harvard Business Press Review.

"HEW News" Office of the Secretary. (1973, March). USPHS Study of untreated syphilis (the Tuskegee Study; Authority to treat participants upon termination of the study). Memorandum from Wilmot R. Hastings to the Secretary.

Kellett, P. M., & Matyok, T. G. (Eds.). (2016). *Transforming conflict through communication in personal, family, and working relationships*. Lexington Books.

Kouzes, J. M., & Posner, B. Z. (2008). *The leadership challenge* (pp. 24-25). Jossey-Bass.

Meacham, J. (2003). *Franklin and Winston: An intimate portrait of an epic friendship*. Random House.

Newell, T., Reeher, G., & Ronayne, P. (2012). *The trusted leader: Building the relationships that make government work* (2nd ed.). CQ Press. https://doi.org/10.4135/9781506335667

NPS. (2015, November). Roosevelt and Churchill: A friendship that saved the world. https://www.nps.gov/articles/fdrww2.htm

Schein, E. H., & Schein, P. A. (2018). *Humble leadership: The power of relationships, openness, and trust*. Berrett-Koehler.

Silver, S. R., & Franz, T. M. (2021). *Meaningful partnership at work: How the workplace covenant ensures mutual accountability and success between leaders and teams*. Productivity Press. https://doi.org/10.4324/9781003181477

Smith, D. M. (2011). *Elephant in the room: How relationships make or break the success of leaders and organizations* (1st ed.). Jossey-Bass.

Vonderlehr, R. A., Clark, T., Wenger, O. C., & Heller, J. R. (1936). Untreated syphilis in the male Negro. *Journal of Venereal Disease Information*.

Young Sheldon. (2017). Chuck Lorre, Bill Prady, Steve Molaro, Todd Spiewak. Watch Young Sheldon | Netflix.

PART 6

WORK WORTH DOING

Not a week goes by without hearing someone talk about retirement and how much longer they have left. American society has taught us to work until a certain age, draw retirement, and do whatever we choose—check off the bucket list. Working people aim to save enough money to relax and do what they have always wanted. Do we work to live or live to work? Do we enjoy what we do, or is it simply a means to meet our needs? Is work a duty or a privilege? The answer to these questions provides a clear view of how we view work. I was shocked the first time I left the United States of America. The work ethic is entirely different: shorter days, longer lunches, and family-oriented environments are what you get in Europe. In one country, everything was done as a family unit or community. There were some excellent takeaways. I wish we could implement them in our work culture.

There is a lot of research on the different generations in the workplace: Silent Generation, Baby Boomers, Generation X, and Generation Y. The names of the generations are based on birth years. The United States and Canada have a difference of two years.[107] The Silent Generation entered the workforce after World War II; they followed a linear career path, had fewer employers, and experienced steady promotions. There was considerable growth in the workforce when the Baby Boomers entered. There were a lot of jobs, and women started to enter the workforce. Gender equality laws, family policies, and workplace conduct came into play. Boomers have stayed in the workforce for the longest period of time. They have changed organizations and careers and occupy the majority of senior positions. Generation X faced a lousy economy when entering the workforce.[108] When the economy improved, they were either too old or lacked experience. They were playing catch up on finding the right fit and careers. As they mature, they slowly move into

---

107 Ng, E. S., Lyons, S. T., & Schweitzer, L. (2018). *Generational Career Shifts: How Matures, Boomers, Gen Xers, and Millennials View Work* (1st ed.). Emerald Publishing Limited. https://doi.org/10.1108/9781787145832
108 Canada Employment Insurance Commission (CEIC). (2009). *Monitoring and assessment report*. Ottawa, Canada: Human Resources and Skills Development Canada.

high-level positions. Many have left organizations to start their own companies because they need more upward mobility. The Millennials were primarily raised in the middle-class culture with post-secondary education and more information than previous generations. They grew up with technology and saw both genders in the workforce.[109] Millennials have seen how technology has shifted jobs and business. They see value in flexibility and meaningful work. Millennials are willing to work for less money and fewer hours to follow what they believe is a world trajectory of harmonious living. Each generation holds different values, attitudes, and career paths regarding work. Other scholars, such as Becton, Walker, & Jones-Farmer, 2014,[110] Costanza, Badger, Fraser, Severt, & Gade, 2012,[111] and Costanza & Finkelstein, 2015[112] believe generational differences are a myth and found no value.

Ng conducted a study in 2018 with over 3,000 participants to see if there were any inter-generational differences in work priorities, career attitudes, experiences, and outcomes. The overall findings of the research revealed significant inter-generational differences:

- The Silent Generations identified with their career while others did not.

- Generation X expressed a greater need to find a work-life balance.

- Millennials placed more emphasis on self-improvement.

109 Foot, D. K., & Stoffman, D. (1996, pg 285-306). *Boom, bust and echo: How to pro fi t from the coming demographic shift. Toronto: MW&R. for job redesign.* Administrative Science Quarterly, 24(2).
110 Becton, J. B., Walker, H. J., & Jones-Farmer, A. (2014). *Generational differences in workplace behavior.* Journal of Applied Social Psychology, 44 (3), 175 À 189.
111 Costanza, D. P., Badger, J. M., Fraser, R. L., Severt, J. B., & Gade, P. A. (2012). *Generational differences in work-related attitudes: A meta-analysis.* Journal of Business and Psychology, 27 (4), 375 À 394.
112 Costanza, D. P., & Finkelstein, L. M. (2015). *Generationally based differences in the workplace: Is there a there there?* Industrial and Organizational Psychology, 8 (3), 308 À 323.

While there are different views on the value of generational work studies, people are frequently switching careers, and to retain employees, organizations will need to create mobility.

Leaders will need to get creative in how they structure their organizations and positions. Researchers found that Generation X was the most unsatisfied group. They are the most critical of how organizations are running and require more work-life balance. The Millennials have the lowest level of career identification. Their expectation of starting points and salary are unrealistic. The workplace had its challenges, still has its challenges, and will continue to have challenges if we do not change how we view work. Meeting everyone's needs takes work, but it is achievable.

There are many elements regarding work and how it has changed over time—early mornings and late nights, from plowing work to computer-operated work. What is work? Webster defines *work* as an activity involving mental or physical effort to achieve a purpose or result; a task or tasks to be undertaken.[113] Work can be associated with meaning and social engagement, which translates to improved health and psychological well-being.[114] Jewish philosophy of work is that every man must have an honest trade to support themselves. Other religious cultures view work as a means to sustain a certain standard of living. Work is a divine service, a laboring of love to others. People need to work in the framework of their gifts. I do not care for fishing much, or the beach for that matter. Working as a fisherman, oceanographer, lifeguard, marine biologist, or diver would be dreadful for me. My performance ratings would be average. I would go through phases throughout the year, dreading going in and looking for the next vacation or holiday. Someone who loves the ocean would enjoy some of those careers and not see it as mere work but a service of love.

113 "work." 2023. In Merriam-Webster.com. Retrieved November 27, 2023, from https:// www.merriam-webster.com/dictionary/work

114 Heaven, B.E.N.; Brown, L.J.; White, M.; Errington, L.; Mathers, J.C.; & Moffatt, S. (2013, pg 91, 222-287). *Supporting well-being in retirement through meaningful social roles: Systematic review of intervention studies.* Milbank Q.

Throughout history, the meaning of work has changed. In the eighth century, Hesiod, a Greek author, wrote that work was for monetary gain and that the gods used humans to work for punishment.[115] Plato taught that human souls were eternal and nourishing the soul meant engaging in proper work (427-347). Greek thinking became a variance to the meaning of work superiority of intellectual work over manual labor.[116] A philosopher in the fifth century taught that work has three values: self-supporting, giving to those in need, and forming holiness.[117] Other philosophers agreed with the three values of work and instructed that work was to be a daily part of life unless one was sick or had something of greater importance that would prevent them from their duties.[118] There are a lot of things to consider when it comes to work. Ancient philosophers believed that work is not a cause for religious perspective but a human ability to be responsible. We are made to work to serve one another, to help our economies grow and flourish. We are led to believe that work is based on social class. What we do for our careers is based on passion. When we take the leap of faith to work in the areas of love and gifting, the dynamics of organizations will change drastically.

I know what you are thinking: there may be jobs someone does not want to do. A person is specially made to do every job we need for the functioning of our society. In the next seven days, we will dive into the meaning and fulfillment of work. Individuals and leaders must understand that the concept of work matters. Leaders will be able to help employees who may not perform well in their area and help them find what they are good at, rather than simply sending them on their way or allowing the organization, customers, and themselves to suffer. If we can transform our thinking on labor, the intent, and the benefits, we can change our organizations.

---

115 Ostring, E. E. (2016). *Be a blessing: the theology of work in the narrative of Genesis.* Wipf & Stock.
116 Ostring, E. E. (2016).
117 Kaiser, E., Theology of Work, 108–19.
118 Placher, Callings, 128; Benedict, Rule of St Benedict.

DAY 1

Have you ever heard someone say that they had a bad day? My daughter, such a sweetie-pie, would make this statement. I would remind her that she did not have a bad day; she just had a bad moment. The day was still ongoing, and she would explain why it was not so great. Again, it was just a moment in time. At the end of the conversation, I would advise her not to stress over the things she cannot control. People spend far too much time worrying, stressing, and panicking about things that do not matter. Your attitude matters—your work ethic matters. Both of them have an internal and external effect. How you show up each day at your workplace affects people's moments. What are my emotions telling me if I had a heated discussion with my husband and came to work without taking the proper time to process what was said, and I knocked everything off the desk just because a pen was out of place? I would be making other people feel my frustrations, which is unwarranted. Or what if I dislike my job, my hours, and the locations; my work could be better, I'm barely showing up on time, my deliverables are late, and I spend more time figuring out how to get out rather than just doing the work? Each example affects me and others. One study showed that a lack of control in the workplace was found to be the number one stressor.[119]

---

119 Karasek, R. (1979). *Job demands, job decision latitude, and mental strain: Implications.*

In Western culture, you can control where you work. If you do not like it, get out of the way, and do it quickly. A poor attitude is like a plague; it can spread rapidly. Perhaps you started off enjoying the work and the organization, but the joy faded over time. There is no harm in not enjoying your work; again, emotions provide us with information. What is done with the information is what matters. We go through seasons, like the Earth-Sun relationship that is responsible for seasons and biodiversity. Work is a part of who we are, and as we evolve, so does our passion and grace. I realized that for my life, I had to be in tune with my emotions because I can become bored with work after a while. I would start to ask myself, "Is it time to move on?" I have a strong work ethic, and I always show up ready to get things done. I was good at my job, but I no longer enjoyed it. I did not sit around and complain for months and years. I made a move to leave graciously into another area. People did not understand. They tried to convince me to stay, made promises, and some tried to instill fear in me because of the fear they had about me leaving. I have done this many times and have realized the grace to do this is no longer there.

The first time I had to leave a job, it could have gone better. I was kicking and screaming because I was performing well. I was comfortable, respected, valued, and had a career plan. My adult tantrums did not go over well. Everyone felt it: my family, colleagues, friends, grocery store clerk, hairdresser...everyone. Lesson learned—not again. Attitude is crucial to the quality of our work life.[120] Do not get me wrong. There are difficult people, but your attitude will determine whether their behavior continues or stops. We teach people how to treat us, be it a colleague, boss, family member, or friend.

Too much stress in the workplace can cause health issues.[121] The stress can lead to meltdowns, depression, or ulcers. Why the stress? There needs to be more connection between our

120 Sessa, V. I., & Bowling, N. A. (Eds.) (2021). *Essentials of job attitudes and other workplace psychological constructs.* Routledge.
121 Greenberg, J. (2004, pg 352-365). *Stress fairness to fare no stress: Managing workplace stress by promoting organizational justice.* Organizational Dynamics, 33(4).

purpose in work and the changing seasons. Why do leaders feel the need to micromanage control? Why do leaders instill fear to feel empowered? Why do leaders try to do everything and have a fear of losing everything? Why do leaders apply undue stress when they are stressed and unhappy? When these things happen, the employee either flees or models the same behavior. The cycle continues unless someone is willing to get off the merry-go-round. A crucial conversation must occur when we witness or behave in these ways. Assess your emotions and where they are stemming from. If we are honest with ourselves, it is not them but "me." No one can take me away my joy and fulfillment in life. It may be time to serve someplace else.

Exercise

Meditate: I cannot control the world. I can control my attitude and work ethic.

Observe: How do I show up to work? Are people running from me or toward me? Am I complaining or appreciative?

Commit: Ask myself, "Is it time to go? Do I enjoy the work I am currently doing?"

DAY 2

"The only way to do great work is to love what you do."
— **Steve Jobs**

Loving what you do makes a world of difference. You may have heard famous people say in interviews that they stopped loving what they were doing after not hearing from them for years. Love is a deep interpersonal affection. The Greek philosophers identified six forms of love[122]:

1. Storge: familial (family) love, a natural affection towards parents or family members.

2. Philia: friendly or platonic love.

3. Eros: romantic love, passionate and/ or sexual love toward a person. The term erotic comes from eros.

4. Philautia: self-love, a basic human necessity for one's happiness. Greeks saw this as a moral flaw. In the 20th century, self-love has taken a positive approach, seen as valuing yourself.

5. Xenia: guest love, a Greek moral obligation to show hospitality towards guests. A relationship of gift exchange, generosity, and reciprocity through material items, shelter, favors, and protection.

6. Agape: divine or unconditional love, the highest form of charity, to hold one in high esteem. In the Christian culture, agape is the love from God to man and man to God. The love is reciprocal. Agape does not look at the conduct of man.

Talking about love and work, some would say they do not go together in the workplace. How is this possible when organiza-

---

122 Ogden, D. (2007). *A companion to Greek religion.* Blackwell Pub. OCLC 173354759.

tions are made up of human beings? Love is having compassion, a connection, gentleness, and tenderness toward others. Employees who feel they work in loving, caring environments report higher job satisfaction and teamwork.[123] Love is all-encompassing and inclusive.

The societal system has taught us to give ourselves to work that will pay us for quality of life. I am not against work, but I have concluded that fulfillment of purpose is not found in just working to live. People are disgruntled, frustrated, depressed, and overwhelmed because they do not love their work. I am talking from the top down. Witherington says, "The most miserable thing a human can experience is the feeling of not knowing what they ought to be doing with their life."[124] If we focus on purpose first, passion second, and then unconditional love, we will see a paradigm shift in the workplace. Jobs was fired from something he loved. He sat around for some months doing nothing. He got himself together and started another company doing what he loved. Jobs did not go to another organization to make money for his lifestyle or fit societal norms. He knew his purpose and was on a continual pursuit.

Work has room for love. Love has room for work. You ought to love what you do. CEOs worth billions of dollars share what leaders should prioritize in the workplace: trust, authenticity, innovation, and a caring culture. Organizations must create a world in which people's lives are full of purpose, creativity, and love.[125] There is an excitement each day when one loves what they do. There are challenges, but they enjoy discovering solutions to sharpen their skills and better understand the industry. To find oneself is to find love; to find love is to find work.

---

123 Barsade, S. G., & O'Neill, O. A. (2014, pg 551-598). *What's Love Got to Do with It? A Longitudinal Study of the Culture of Companionate Love and Employee and Client Outcomes in a Long-term Care Setting.* Administrative Science Quarterly, 59(4). https://doi.org/10.1177/0001839214538636
124 Witherington, B. (2011). *Work: A kingdom perspective on labor.* Wm. B. Eerdmans Publishing Co.
125 Mackey, J. & Sisodia, R. (2013). *"Conscious Capitalism" is not an oxymoron.* Harvard Business Review. https://hbr.org/2013/01/cultivating-a-higher-conscious

Exercise

Meditate: There is purpose, passion, creativity, and love in me.

Observe: Do I love what I do?

Commit: Love myself and others unconditionally.

DAY 3

"There are certain things that are fundamental to human fulfillment. The essence of these needs is captured in the phrase 'to live, to love, to learn, to leave a legacy.' The need to leave a legacy is our spiritual need to have a sense of meaning, purpose, personal congruence, and contribution."
— **Stephen Covey**

I have been a cashier, sandwich maker, fry dropper, drive-thru clerk, sales associate, truck driver, secretary, administrator, care-taker, babysitter, organizer, counselor, coach, instructor, train-er, facilitator, program manager, project manager, chauffeur, group leader, editor, seamstress, content creator, and an advo-cate. There was a time in each of these jobs when I learned a new skill and something about myself. At the beginning of those jobs, I was excited and could not wait to start my day. Over time, the pure joy of doing the job was lost, like a balloon slipping out of a child's hands. Those times of employment were all part of my journey in life. There was harmony; I was not forced or coerced into taking any of those jobs. I jumped right into them of my own accord. Why did I leave those jobs? I got bored, or I had outgrown them.

A study on job satisfaction among American workers was done in 2005. Over 33 percent of the 10,000 employees sur-veyed said they were under-stimulated.[126] In 2021, job satisfac-tion was higher and is still slowly climbing, but steadily. The significant difference is that individuals have and are switching jobs. There was a big shift in career moves and entrepreneur-

126 Malachowski, D. (2005). *Wasted Time At Work Costing Companies Billions.* www.salary.com/careers/layouthtmls/crel_display_nocat_Ser374_Par555.html

ship post-pandemic. The report's lowest components were (in sequential order): promotion policy, bonus plan, educational/ job training programs, recognition, performance review, and retirement plan. Kant believes that humans are the only ones with a need for work. He argues that amusement cannot fulfill this function; if a person tries, they will feel lifeless.[127]

Employees become bored when they are doing meaningless tasks or when they are under-stimulated by an organizational problem. How often have you met about the same thing or found yourself doing the same work? How many times have we started things and left them unfinished, only to come back to them one or two years later as if it were a new idea? How many times have we created PowerPoint slides about the same things? How many times have we done work that another team or business unit is doing or has already done? And we think people will not get bored. Later on in my journey, I realized that I do not do well in repetitive environments. To be effective, I need stimulation to my brain, critical thinking, creating, failing, and discovering. Have you felt the work days were long and the weekend goes by too fast? There are 24 hours a day; nothing has changed. Time goes by fast when you are doing things you love and enjoy. The difference in the examples is that some found meaning in their work, and others did not.

Svendsen brings up an interesting point: if there is meaning in work, then there is meaningless work.[128] There is work that has more meaning than others. I do not know if we can hold this to be true. After all, isn't beauty in the eyes of the beholder? Is a family doctor more important than a surgeon, a psychiatrist, a little league coach, or a sales representative more important than an intelligence operation officer? It is important for each individual to find meaning in those areas. One cannot say their child is more important than someone else's child.

There is a parable about two women who come to the king. Two babies of the same sex were born around the same time.

127 Kant, I. (1803, 1902–) *Pädagogik. In Kants gesammelte Schriften, vol. VII.* Berlin: de Gruyter.
128 Svendsen, L. Fr. H. (2014). *Work.* Routledge. https://doi.org/10.4324/9781315710327

LEADERSHIP EVOLUTION

One of the babies dies during the night. The mother whose child dies takes the living child and places the child who has died with the other woman. When the woman wakes up, she notices the child is dead and that the child is not hers. She confronts the other mother, and they end up in the king's court. They go back and forth about whose child it is; the king suggests a solution: "Bring me my sword, cut the child in half! That way, each of you can have part of him." The king knew this would kill the child. The baby's mother screamed, "Please do not kill my son! I love him very much. Give him to her. Just do not kill him." The other told the king to go ahead and cut him in half so neither of them would have him. The king pointed to the first woman and said, "She is the real mother; give him to her." (1 Kings 3:16-18). Meaning is found in the one who finds it meaningful.

Find meaning in the work you do, whether you get paid for it or not. There were times when the job I did was merely a job. However, I simultaneously found meaningful work until I could move from the job. I volunteer a lot, and I found meaning in those areas. We may need to come to terms with our vocation, which might be free; it feeds the heart.[129] I do not entirely disagree with Taylor; we need to feed our hearts, and if we had more faith, those things could provide us with the quality of life we desire.

Exercise

Meditate: Meaningfulness of work is what I believe to be meaningful.

Observe: What work feeds my heart?

Commit: Find meaning that feeds the heart and do it regardless of monetary gain.

---

129 Taylor, B. B. (2009). *An Altar in the World*. HarperCollins.

DAY 4

"The world is changed by your example, not by your opinion"
— **Paulo Coelho**

People do too much talking. One of my mottos is, "I can show you better than I can tell you." There needs to be more doers in this world. Modeling is a powerful tool; whether we want the job or not, we are modeling before others. One reason I took leading myself as a personal mission to discovery, understanding, clarity, and development in leadership is the principle of modeling. I modeled some of my leaders, but it did not go well for me. If I could go back and do it all over again, I would. I am grateful that the people I was leading did not tie me up like a sacrificial meal in the wilderness. In the book *"The Leadership Challenge: How to Make Extraordinary Things Happen in Organizations"* by James Kouzes and Barry Posner, there is a chapter on *"Modeling the Way."* The chapter speaks on two main points:[130]

1. Clarifying values by finding your voice and affirming shared values.

People want to know who you are. What are your values, beliefs, ethics, standards, and ideas? I have sat through many inauguration speeches in different organizations. These are some of the most critical moments of a leader's time. Employees sit in anticipation, waiting to hear that a savior has come to save, deliver, and set them free. Okay, maybe that sounds a bit dramatic, but they do want to know what the leader believes in, what new things they will do, and how they will fit into these

---

130 Kouzes, J. M., & Posner, B. Z. (2017). *The leadership challenge: How to make extraordinary things happen in organizations (6th ed.).*

ideas. When the speech is magical, people walk away saying, "Hmmm…we will see. So and so already promised that, and it did not happen." When the speech is empty and unclear, people walk away saying, "Who hired them? We are in trouble. It might be time to start looking for another job." Whether it was good or bad, the words spoken have gone into the ear gates of human beings, and they will hold you accountable. As a leader, you must realize that you are not just speaking for yourself when discussing values and principles. You are speaking on behalf of the whole organization. It is no longer "I" but "we."[131] People need to know the person behind the microphone. It would be best to express your authentic self when communicating your beliefs.

Understand your leadership philosophy. You must find your voice before you can become a credible leader by connecting what you say to what you do. I had other voices saying what I wanted to hear, so I copied their words and tone, which made it challenging to stay true to them. When I wanted to be compassionate, the words I spoke said otherwise. I had to find my philosophy in what I believe to be true in leading others. You will not have the integrity to lead when you cannot keep your word.[132] Being someone else is exhausting.

2. Setting the examples by aligning actions with shared values.

Leadership is not a play where you get to put on a different persona. Leadership is an artful lifestyle. Who you are will determine the type of art individuals will experience. Utilizing other people's names to get things done is not leading. Knowing why you joined the organization will help put words to action. As a child, I had no problems keeping a clean space. I would clean my two sisters' area when I could no longer take the clutter. My mother did not have to get on me because we shared the same values in cleanliness. As we got older, I did not use "Mom said" to get them to clean. I used the tactic, "If we want

---

131 Kouzes, J. M., & Posner, B. Z. (2017). *The leadership challenge: How to make extraordinary things happen in organizations* (6th ed.).
132 Kouzes, J. M., & Posner, B. Z. (2017).

to go, we need to clean," and it worked. My daughter has yet to take on this value. My sisters would vote for me (2:1) to ask to go places until I started to say, "No, you go ask for yourself." You cannot lead through others or their experience. You have to know what works for you.

A study was conducted to see if personal values made a difference in how people behave in the workplace. The study showed that when managers were unclear about their personal or organizational values, the level of commitment was low. Managers who were clear in both personal and organizational values had higher commitment levels.[133]

People need to have a reason to care about what they are doing. There is no undue stress; work must be done effectively. Have you ever been on a team where everything just flowed? You were happy when you got home, happy to go back in, you could not wait to go over ideas with the team, and in the end, you wanted to hang on to the engagement, excitement, commitment, and drive. I once saw a group of seasoned men, about five or six, having lunch, and you could tell they had been friends for years. Their energy and display of affection in public fascinated me so much that I wanted to change seats. I left the restaurant thinking how wonderful it is to have a strong relationship that keeps you together over the years. Those men chose to go through life together, and they happened to meet at work.

Employees value advancement, social interaction at work, prestigious work, and influence.[134] Shared values are beliefs people hold true to themselves; they are not catchphrases to get likes and followers. These values influence how people do their job. Take off the other person's clothes and wear those that fit you well. Know what you believe so you can do what you say.

---

133 Posner, Barry Z. (2010, pg 535-541). *Another look at the impact of personal and organizational values congruency.* Journal of Business Ethics 97.

134 Ng, E. S., Lyons, S. T., & Schweitzer, L. (2018). *Generational Career Shifts: How Matures, Boomers, Gen Xers, and Millennials View Work (1st ed.).* Emerald Publishing Limited. https://doi.org/10.1108/9781787145832

Exercise

Meditate: Find my voice so that it aligns with my words and deeds.

Observe: Do I know my values? Is it hard to do what I say?

Commit: Identify my values, talk about what is important to me, and create a space for others to do the same.

DAY 5

Getting an adolescent to take out the trash is like teaching a turtle to climb a tree. In their eyes, taking the trash out has no relevance to their life. The trash is unimportant until they hear those famous words, "Didn't I tell you to get the trash out?" or suddenly, the game system stops working, and they crawl out from their world to ask what happened. Your response was, "It must have been the trash police," knowing you were the one who turned off the Wi-Fi on their device. The importance of work is the value we consciously decide as individuals. It is important not to define yourself by what you do. I call this the "identity crisis stage"; what you do is not who you are. You have had at least two jobs by now. Are you a cashier, business owner, artist, or singer? Those are functions, not being. Can you describe who you are in five or fewer words? People have identified with a role in which they do not know who they are without it. This is why we have individuals sitting in positions for over 20, 30, and 40 years. People leave organizations because there is no upward mobility—the reason why America is not leading in innovation. People are afraid to be sensitive to knowing when it is time to leave. I applaud leaders who know when to move on, even when others try to hold on.

Karen, a senior leader, did a performance review with Debbie. Debbie was a great employee. Karen gave her a rave review, encouraged her to continue developing, and then told her she was no longer needed. Debbie was shocked and confused.

She asked Karen why she was fired if she did such a great job. Karen told Debbie it would be selfish of her to keep her there. She encouraged Debbie to fulfill her purpose. Debbie was upset and angry with Karen. I was shocked to hear this story. What kind of leader is so settled in who they are that they would let go of someone who was making their team shine? What kind of leader is selfless enough to recognize that they are hindering someone's growth? Karen had courage and love for her employees to do what she did. In a few months, Debbie called back to thank Karen for firing her because she would have never been where she was. How many of us are like Debbie and holding onto what we have because we've decided it makes us who we are? The world evolves, and we as humans evolve too, whether we like it or not. For example, did you have hair on your head at ten years old, but at 60, you joined the baldy club? Debbie did great work, but she also was not aligned with her purpose.

The book "The Purpose Driven Life," written by Rick Warren, is a 40-day personal spiritual journey of what Rick believes God has given humans life on Earth. Although the book is based on the Christian faith, other religious leaders have found it helpful. The book topped the *Wall Street Journal's* best seller chart and stayed on the *New York Bestseller* list for over 90 weeks. Warren says envy and people-pleasing are the two biggest reasons people do not live purpose-driven lives. I am not here to convert you; I am here to point you in a different way that will bring you results. We do not know what we do not know. I have held over fifteen jobs, none of which define my identity.

We spend our whole lives trying to discover purpose, as there is a misconception that it can be one thing when it can be many—envy, looking at what others are doing and setting out to do the same. I struggled in this area. I often looked at others and said, "God, why didn't you give me that idea?" It was challenging to let go of the idea of others' lives and success and walk on my path. I was Debbie, doing it well, a performer, a finisher. I had to ask myself the tricky question: Why are you doing this? When I could answer the question honestly, my outlook on life shifted in many ways. While you are on the path of discovery, actively moving forward, do it well. My mother would say, "If you are not going to do it right, do not do it at all; now get out of the way."

"Being successful and fulfilling life's purpose are not the same," Rick states.

Exercise

Meditate: My role is not my identity.

Observe: What drives my life?

Commit: Whatever I decide to do, do it well.

DAY 6

"People often say that motivation doesn't last. Well, neither does bathing. That's why we recommend it daily."
— **Zig Ziglar**

How you perceive your work is how you will respond in performance. Motivation comes from within; it is a choice. Lack of motivation is evident in how a person moves throughout the day. Interestingly, management is surprised when someone gives a two-week notice to leave the organization. Every organization has an opportunity to make a great workplace. Who is responsible? Leaders. The challenge leaders face is getting in their own way. Walter Robb, Co-CEO of Whole Foods Market, dislikes it when people do not take responsibility, stating, "It should be about what you can do, not what you cannot do." Creating a great workplace is not straightforward, but it is doable. The question is, do leaders want to do it? The list of the 100 best companies to work for is not exclusive. Leaders from these organizations are saying the same things: they avoid cognitive obstacles; success is a product of hard work, not luck or chance; they avoid over-generalizing and are not seduced by best practices that do not work for them, and they take the long route instead of shortcuts.[135] I have seen organizational leaders deploy campaigns and task forces intending to improve the workplace and get more engagement with little traction over time. It is the big shiny toy under the Christmas tree, and after a week, the toy is nowhere to be found. Creating an environment of value, trust, love, and joy will only be achieved by making it

---

135 Robin, J., & Burchell, M. (2013). *No excuses: how you can turn any workplace into a great one (First edition).* Jossey-Bass.

part of the organization's identity. Until it becomes a part of the vision, it is here today and gone tomorrow.

What one truly cares about will manifest in their actions. Leaders must show up each day believing in the vision of the organization. In 2020, The State of Leadership Development surveyed 21,008 employees to assess leaders' effectiveness. In the Leadership IQ report released, the organization's vision is misaligned with leaders. 29% of employees have said their leader's vision aligned with the organization.[136] Leaders have to take responsibility for the chaos in day-to-day operations. The pandemic has been an eye-opener for many people; why should they deal with confusion, disorganization, and repetitive rework? People spend the majority of their waking hours working. They do not want the stress that is created because of laziness. There is a cost to success, and many of us want to avoid paying the price. You hear the stories of the sleepless nights of top organizations making the top 100 list. However, we fail to realize and be at peace that it will not last forever. Everything, and I mean everything, has a season. A woman does not stay pregnant for the rest of her life, nor does a baby stay an infant forever. Those beginning stages will be rough. You may eventually achieve something great, but it will take work to get there. Otherwise, there is no appreciation. Take it from a person who experienced times without running water and homelessness. I appreciate having water and a safe place to lay my head.

Three issues keep leaders from having enough time, energy, and skills.[137] Who has enough time? Why do you think the concept of "use or lose and carry-over hours for leave" has come into play? Hewlett & Luce found that the American dream was extreme in 2006. They noted, "62% of high-earning individuals work more than 50 hours a week, 35% work more than 60

---

136 *The State of Leadership Development Report.* Harvard Business Publishing. (2023, January 23). https://www.harvardbusiness.org/insight/the-state-of-leadership-development-report/
137 Robin, J., & Burchell, M. (2013). *No excuses: how you can turn any workplace into a great one (First edition).* Jossey-Bass.

hours a week, and 10% work more than 80 hours a week."[138] People who wanted to be at the top worked well over 70 hours a week. The way we work has changed, but there still are some extremes. I can see why leaders may not be motivated to work for a great workplace. Robin suggests ways for leaders to change how they look at making great workplaces:

1. Do not create anything new. Change how you do what you already do. For example, take lunch breaks with employees to talk with them and allow them to ask questions.

2. Prioritize your culture; that is the primary function of your job.

3. Work hard to ensure the short-term pressure does not pull you back into the lousy workplace habits.

Motivation is a daily vitamin to leading and the organization's wealth. Do not leave home or start your day without it. All things are possible if you are willing to work and love what you do.

Exercise

Meditate: For great workplaces to exist, I have to bring value, trust, and love to work.

Observe: Does my vision align with the organization?

Commit: Value people.

---

138 Hewlett, Sylvia Ann, and Carolyn Buck Luce. (2006, pg. 49-59). *Extreme Jobs—The Dangerous Allure of the 70-Hour Workweek.* Harvard Business Review 84, no. 12.

DAY 7

Take some time today to reflect on the past six days.

- How do you feel about work?
- What types of jobs have you had over the years?
- Which one brought you the most fulfillment and why?
- Do you enjoy what you do?
- Do you enjoy the people you work with?

The Earth cannot survive without the work of human beings. We can do beautiful things to enhance the Earth, or we can do things to harm it. There isn't just one thing we are meant to do in life. We search and search for our purpose, and we miss the discovery and the enjoyment of life along the way. We tend to remain idle because a lion may be out there, and we fear that we might die. We will die one day, but who is to say today is the day? No one knows the day or hour we will leave this world. Every day you wake up, see it as a new opportunity to experience something different. Refrain from wasting time or energy under the pressure of the misconception of societal beliefs in work. People spend too many hours figuring out how to get out of work when they have created another job.

Loving what you do makes a world of difference. Seeing the value in others makes a difference. Work is a service to others. No matter the service or the season of life you are in, do what you are doing and do it well. There will always be someone smarter, faster, better looking, wealthier, stronger, bigger, smaller, who cooks better, or who dances better. What does this have to do with who you are and what you were created for?

Let us embrace all people: sex, race, gender, sexual orientation, disabilities, and generational differences. The task of all human beings is to love others as we love ourselves. Do not assume that there is only one vocation for life. We need to have flexibility and openness to see other possibilities. Witherington says we are to ask ourselves these questions when it comes to life work:

- What will our legacy be?
- How would you want your work to be assessed by God and people?
- How does your work foreshadow?

Work does not have to be laborious and grueling. The work we do should bring us joy. You have the power to make culture and to leave a legacy. Few have found the blessings of working to make a difference, not just an income. I encourage you to take a leap of faith to trust those calls of doing what brings you joy. Everyone deserves a workplace filled with joy.

References

Barsade, S. G., & O'Neill, O. A. (2014). What's love got to do with it? A longitudinal study of the culture of companionate love and employee and client outcomes in a long-term care setting. *Administrative Science Quarterly, 59*(4), 551-598. https://doi.org/10.1177/0001839214538636

Becton, J. B., Walker, H. J., & Jones-Farmer, A. (2014). Generational differences in workplace behavior. *Journal of Applied Social Psychology, 44*(3), 175-189.

Canada Employment Insurance Commission (CEIC). (2009). *Monitoring and assessment report.* Ottawa, Canada: Human Resources and Skills Development Canada.

Costanza, D. P., & Finkelstein, L. M. (2015). Generationally based differences in the workplace: Is there a there there? *Industrial and Organizational Psychology, 8*(3), 308-323.

Costanza, D. P., Badger, J. M., Fraser, R. L., Severt, J. B., & Gade, P. A. (2012). Generational differences in work-related attitudes: A meta-analysis. *Journal of Business and Psychology, 27*(4), 375-394.

English Standard Version. (2019). *Bible Gateway.* www.biblegateway.com.

Foot, D. K., & Stoffman, D. (1996). *Boom, bust and echo: How to profit from the coming demographic shift.* Toronto: MW&R.

Greenberg, J. (2004). Stress fairness to fare no stress: Managing workplace stress by promoting organizational justice. *Organizational Dynamics, 33*(4), 352-365.

Hall, W. (1844). *An address delivered August 14, 1844: Before the Society of Phi Beta Kappa in Yale College.* Harvard University: B. L. Hamlen.

Heaven, B. E. N., Brown, L. J., White, M., Errington, L., Mathers, J. C., & Moffatt, S. (2013). Supporting well-being in retirement through meaningful social roles: Systematic review of intervention studies. *Milbank Quarterly, 91*, 222-287.

Hesiod. (1914). *Works and Days.*

Hewlett, S. A., & Luce, C. B. (2006). Extreme jobs–The dangerous allure of the 70-hour workweek. *Harvard Business Review, 84*(12), 49–59.

Job Satisfaction 2023 Report. (2023). *The Conference Board.* https://www.conference-board.org/pdfdownload.cfm?masterProductID=46114

Kaiser Jr, W. C. (2009). *The promise-plan of God: A biblical theology of the Old and New Testaments.* Zondervan Academic.

Kant, I. (1902). *Pädagogik. In Kants gesammelte Schriften, Vol. VII.* Berlin: de Gruyter. (Original work published 1803)

Karasek, R. (1979). Job demands, job decision latitude, and mental strain: Implications for job redesign. *Administrative Science Quarterly, 24*(2), 285–306.

Kouzes, J. M., & Posner, B. Z. (2017). *The leadership challenge: How to make extraordinary things happen in organizations* (6th ed.).

Mackey, J., & Sisodia, R. (2013, January 14). "Conscious Capitalism" is not an oxymoron. *Harvard Business Review.* https://hbr.org/2013/01/cultivating-a-higher-conscious

Malachowski, D. (2005). Wasted time at work costing companies billions. *Salary.com.* www.salary.com/careers/layouthtmls/crel_display_nocat_Ser374_Par555.html

Matz-Costa, C., Besen, E., Boone James, J., & Pitt-Catsouphes, M. (2012). Differential impact of multiple levels of productive activity engagement on psychological well-being in middle and later life. *Gerontologist, 54*, 277-289.

Ng, E. S., Lyons, S. T., & Schweitzer, L. (2018). *Generational career shifts: How matures, boomers, Gen Xers, and millennials view work* (1st ed.). Emerald Publishing Limited. https://doi.org/10.1108/9781787145832

Ogden, D. (2007). *A companion to Greek religion.* Blackwell Pub. OCLC 173354759.

Ostring, E. E. (2016). *Be a blessing: The theology of work in the narrative of Genesis.* Wipf & Stock.

Placher, W. C. (Ed.). (2005). *Callings: Twenty centuries of Christian wisdom on vocation.* Eerdmans.

Posner, B. Z. (2010). Another look at the impact of personal and organizational values congruency. *Journal of Business Ethics, 97*(4), 535-541.

Robin, J., & Burchell, M. (2013). *No excuses: How you can turn any workplace into a great one* (1st ed.). Jossey-Bass.

Sessa, V. I., & Bowling, N. A. (Eds.). (2021). *Essentials of job attitudes and other workplace psychological constructs.* Routledge.

Svendsen, L. F. H. (2014). *Work.* Routledge. https://doi.org/10.4324/9781315710327

Taylor, B. B. (2009). *An altar in the world.* HarperCollins.

Warren, R. (2013). *What on earth am I here for?* Zondervan.

Witherington, B. (2011). *Work: A kingdom perspective on labor.* Wm. B. Eerdmans Publishing Co.

Work. (2023). In *Merriam-Webster.com.* Retrieved November 27, 2023, from https://www.merriam-webster.com/dictionary/work

The State of Leadership Development Report. (2023, January 23). *Harvard Business Publishing.* https://www.harvardbusiness.org/insight/the-state-of-leadership-development-report/

PART 7

GROWING
TOGETHER

Do you want to grow? Develop yourself first. Do you want to lead? Develop others. Being a personal master of anything in life will take intentional time and effort. Practice does not make perfect. Practice builds confidence and effective results. Statistics show that individuals who are experts and elite performers in a field have spent at least 10,000 hours over the course of 10 years studying with devoted teachers, coaches, or mentors, supported by family and friends.[139] There is intentionality in working daily. It makes a person better and assured in their actions. They seek feedback so they can adjust themselves as needed. Feedback is critical in the learning process. We may see or feel ourselves doing certain things that are not complete. When learning a dance routine, you intentionally follow someone else. When you do it independently, you need a mirror or someone else watching to tell whether your arm, leg, shoulders, feet, or hips are appropriately placed in each step. Why is it important to develop ourselves first? As a leader, you will challenge others to grow, develop, and become a better version of themselves. How can you require growth from others if you are unwilling to go first?

The more time you spend with others, the more you discover differences and similarities within yourself. There are different skills, strengths, weaknesses, backgrounds, and personalities. People will not do things exactly like you because you are you, and they are them. We do not often consider the growth of people's minds as we consider the growth of their skills; both types of growth play a vital part in a person's success and effectiveness.[140] It is easier for us to understand a baby's growth process compared to that of an adult. Kegan, a William and Miriam Meehan Professor of Adult Learning and Professional Development at the Harvard Graduate School of Education, speaks on the mental complexity of adulthood. He states that our cul-

139 Ericsson, K.A., Prietula, M.J. and Cokely, E.T. (2007). *The making of an expert.* Harvard Business Review. Available from: https://hbr.org/2007/07/the-making-of-an-expert. Accessed December 5, 2023.
140 Garvey Berger, J (2011). *Changing on the Job: Developing Leaders for a Complex World (1st ed.).* Stanford University Press.

ture must be a place of good learning. There must be a challenging curriculum that also provides the guidance and support needed to master the course.[141] People react to the same situation differently. Self-complexity is also referred to as "forms of mind" or "action logics" of understanding the complex world around us.[142] Some have developed self-complexity, and others have yet to arrive. Kegan and other scholars are not saying that some adults are not intelligent. They point out that we all arrive at self-complexity at different times and in different ways. As a leader, having an excellent capacity for self-complexity is vital. You will encounter situations, different personalities, and challenges from your team; they will challenge you.

The leader must be committed to personal development in order to develop others. Leaders primarily model development. Followers will model values, identity, emotions, and motives based on their leadership. Self-awareness gains clarity in concordance with core values and makes meaning of the world around us.[143] Leaders should be a positive role model for leaders. Fazio lists different areas where a leader develops others by affirming, gratitude, justifying, opportunity, blessings, and focus.[144] Here are a few examples of positive versus negative leaders.

Negative Leaders	Positive Leaders
Focus on who they can blame when things go wrong.	Believe people come to work to do a good job. They tell others "Thank you" regularly for their contributions.
Try to get people to do things that they do not want or like.	They validate the reasons why individuals are on the team.

141 Kegan, R. (1994). *In over our heads: The mental demands of modern life.* Harvard University Press.

142 Garvey Berger, J (2011). *Changing on the Job: Developing Leaders for a Complex World (1st ed.).* Stanford University Press.

143 Gardner, W. L., Avolio, B. J., Luthans, F., May, D. R., & Walumbwa, F. (2005, pg 343-372). *Can you see the real me? A self-based model of authentic leader and follower development.* The Leadership Quarterly, 16(3). https://doi.org/10.1016/j.leaqua.2005.03.003

144 Fazio, Vincent is president of Keystone Leadership Group LLC.

See it as more people, more problems, and more matters to handle.	Welcome others' uniqueness and the value they will bring to the team.

How leaders are developed impacts the culture of organizations. As leaders develop, they are to develop their teams to have a continual flow of positive attitudes instead of negative ones. The development will take work and dedication. Many people join the gym at the beginning of the year, but by February, they are nowhere to be found. John Maxwell says we should look at the development process like investing in the stock market, where "success is not going to happen overnight." People spend a lifetime saving and building up to become wealthy; it is a slow process with significant dividends. Maxwell provides four growth phases: I do not know what I do not know, I know what I do not know, I grow and know, and it starts to show, and I go because of what I know.[145] Leadership is developed daily, not just for one day. People do not want to pay the price, but it will cost you to grow yourself and others. Benjamin Disraeli once said, "The secret of success in life is for a man to be ready for his time when it comes." You cannot wait until the role presents itself; no expert waits until an opportunity presents itself. They practice daily to become proficient.

As we look at the next seven days, remember that there is a law of process. The work you put in; you will get out. If you want to lead the development of yourself and others, you must be ready to put in the work. Leading is not about you; it is about serving others. Development takes a lifetime, so why wait to start?

---

145 Maxwell, J. C. (1998). *The 21 irrefutable laws of leadership: Follow them and people will follow you.* Thomas Nelson.

DAY 1

"Unless you want to carry the whole load yourself,
you need to be developing leaders."
— **John C. Maxwell**

One person cannot do it all. We are individuals who make up a team. We each have different skills, perspectives, experiences, and knowledge. There is no "I" in the word team. I checked. Ants do not have a leader in their colony, so how do they get anything done? A French naturalist named Réaumur was the first to conduct documented studies on ants in the eighteenth century. Réaumur described them as a group of subordinates happy to serve their colony. Within the colony, there are only one or more reproductive females; the rest are sterile.[146] Over time, further discoveries have shown that there are over 11,000 species of ants per colony. They live in female colonies. Some are reproductive, while others are sterile. William used the term "superorganisms" to compare the ant colony to a single organism. The queen and the colony all act as one cell and contribute to the life cycle.[147] Ants do not produce more ants; they reproduce more colonies. Ants rely on chemical cues and perform the same tasks repeatedly. They have glands that secrete these chemicals. Wilson discovered harvester ants treated with oleic acid would go kicking and live. Sometimes, the ant would be taken to the midden.[148] Depending on what the ant was doing, it would determine whether they took the ant with oleic acid to

---

146 Gordon, D. (Deborah M.) (2010). *Ant encounters interaction networks and colony behavior (Course Book)*. Princeton University Press. https://doi.org/10.1515/9781400835447
147 Gordon, D. (Deborah M.) (2010).
148 Wilson, E. O., N. I. Durlach, and L. M. Roth. (1958, pg 108-114). *Chemical releasers of necrophoric behavior in ants*. Psyche 65(4).

the midden. The ants being carried were not dead, just lifeless/motionless and unable to perform their duties.

An ant colony changes over the years as it grows bigger and older. Gordon discovered that ants switch tasks due to environmental changes and interactions with other ants. Ants' behavior is not based on fixed chemical signals.[149] Ants make collective decisions, find resources, move around, and maintain an environment for growth and reproduction patterns. What one ant does will affect all the other ants. When we look at how human beings interact with the Earth, we change the course of how we do things. We intervene in natural processes, such as cloning pigs, vaccinations, artificial fish, manufactured vegetables, or fruits. Human beings came up with these methodologies whereas with ants, there is no innovative way to make more ants or food. The ant is changed by their interaction with another ant. There are 11,000 species, but only 50 have been studied. Some ants fly, watch/track—although they do not have good sight—carry food above their head, and swim with the perfect breaststroke. Ants work hard. They are not lazy creatures; they have a focus and drive to complete their tasks.

The fantastic thing about ants is that there is no hierarchy, and they get more work done than the Armed Forces. We can learn a lot from ants on how to lead others. Leading is not dominating over another, but rather pointing them in the right direction and working together to complete the task. Ants leave the home if there is not enough food. They base their actions and methods on their interactions with one another. They move as a unit, not as individuals. Leaders must look at the development of others as a moving unit. The older ants model behavior for the younger ants. The older ants have a specific job and so do the younger ones. Suppose the younger were to be removed from the colony, the older ants would split their group to fill the gap until the younger ants return.

---

149 Gordon, D. (Deborah M.) (2010). *Ant encounters interaction networks and colony behavior (Course Book).* Princeton University Press. https://doi.org/10.1515/9781400835447

LEADERSHIP EVOLUTION

There is much work to be done, but one person cannot do it all. Developing others allows people to move right into position with no missed deliverables. Nothing should stop because a person went on vacation, is sick, or left the organization. Organizations have not done an excellent job in succession planning. Who can step in your place if an unforeseen event removes you from the office? "Call me on my mobile if you need me" is what we often hear. The problem is that we need to trust the people who work for us and with us. You are one of many who can do the job. The one thing I enjoy about leading is the new challenges. Why? Every encounter with others is an opportunity for growth.

Whether you are in a leading role today or in the future, constantly work to work yourself out of a job. Your skills may have made the position, but your character should grow retention.

Exercise

Meditate: I am not built to carry the load alone.

Observe: How many people from my team can I leave in charge and not be concerned about target dates being missed?

Commit: Develop others in the position I am responsible for. Put a succession plan together and make it public to key people.

DAY 2

"Before you are a leader, success is all about growing yourself.
When you become a leader, success is all about growing others."
—Jack Welch

I have been on a few sports teams growing up. The coach significantly impacted the team on and off the court. The coach provided direction for the sport and life. The way they talked to players helped shape them and develop their character. I remember one particular team, where the coach was not my favorite person. They played favoritism and did not ask how I was doing; it was always about the game. At the time, home life was not great. I was drowning with no outlet. I had a bad attitude; I was angry, hungry, sleepy, and disappointed. No adult around took the time to ask me what was going on. They would punish me by benching me, running extensive laps, and making me clean up after everyone. I came to believe that no one cared about me and that I had to care for myself. You can imagine how off-putting I was with this mentality.

A coach is there to help a person improve in particular areas. A coach provides a safe space and structure for learning and growth. They help with your values and reconnect them to your work. The hours I spent with my coaches were, on average, 2-3 hours per day, depending on the activities. This is around 10 to 15 hours a week. There is no actual scientific data on how long it takes to form a habit, according to the University of Pennsylvania's Wharton Business School.[150] Forming a new habit is up to the person, environment, and habit. Repetition, support, and guidance can move the process forward quickly. A coach is good at their job because they have been there before or immersed themselves in the sport. Molly McGrath, the corporate businesswoman turned high school football coach in the movie *Wildcats*, never played football, but she took a losing high school team to the state championship. Richard Dove Williams Jr. took a few tennis lessons here and there from an older gentleman and decided his two daughters, Serena and Venus Williams, would be professional tennis players. He decided to coach them when he felt the girls were not being coached to their potential.[151]

Leaders are coaches. You can be the coach I had who only cared about the work versus my soul or the coach who develops the player to their full potential. Zenger and Stinnett provide ten things that will change organizations for the better when leaders understand the power of coaching:[152]

1. Bring meaning to work.

2. Have engaged and committed employees.

3. Higher productivity.

4. Stronger culture.

5. Strengthened bonds.

6. Healthier individuals.

7. Resilience.

8. Heightened creativity.

9. Increased risk-taking and exploring.

10. Having a mindset of an owner versus a hired hand.

150 Stillman, J. (2023). *Researchers finally figured out how long it really takes to form a new habit: The often repeated figure of 21 days turns out to be a myth.* https://www.inc.com/jessica-stillman/researchers-finally-figured-out-how-long-it-really-takes-to-form-a-new-habit.html. Accessed December 7, 2023.
151 Williams, R. (2017). *Black and white: The way I see it.* Atria
152 Zenger, J. H. & Stinnett, K. (2010). *The extraordinary coach: how the best leaders help others grow. 1st edition.* McGraw-Hill.

You may have had great coaches in your lifetime and can glean from those experiences or, like me, you may not have had a good experience. Leading requires unlearning old habits, which is more complex than making new ones. It can be hard not to jump in and roll up your sleeves to do the work or give advice. Did your coach play in the game? Most likely, they were not qualified. Leaders have to learn how to get employees to reach their own conclusions. If not, they are hindering their learning. People need to be able to think for themselves. As my daughter gets older, I have found it challenging to let go and allow her to make her own decisions. I realize that if I do not, it will cause a delay in her development. Leaders should not be quick to give advice; they need to take the time to listen. Allow the individual to discuss what is happening and come up with possible resolutions. My calendar might only work for some people to keep them on task.

Leading is developing others to reach their full potential. Remember, it is not about how you played the game because they are not you. Allow them to play to their strengths by guiding them. You might end up jumping over the seats like Mr. Williams dancing because you see all the hard work paid off.

Exercise

Meditate: Solving someone else's problem is a roadblock to their discovery of a resolution.

Observe: Do I listen and ask a lot of questions? Do I offer up advice to quickly get to the next thing? Does the conversation shut down?

Commit: Become curious by asking a lot of questions. Help them to get to the root of the issue and hold them accountable for the actions they said they would do.

DAY 3

*"Treat people as if they were what they ought to be and you help
them to become what they are capable of being."*
— **Johann Wolfgang von Goethe**

There are always two sides to a story. A little girl thought she
was rescuing a beast. The creature thought a beast was kidnap-
ping him. The creature was playing and singing a song, and the
little girl heard a cry for help. The creature had to walk back
and forth for no reason. The little girl gave the beast time to
play and enjoy the fresh air. The story is from the book "The
Tale of Two Beasts" by Fiona Robertson.[153] The little girl and
the creature both saw each other as the beast. The little girl
thought she was helping the beast. The creature thought the
beast was causing him harm. Remember, there are always two
sides to a story. Leaders must be willing to see things from a
different perspective. Although a person may behave a certain
way, can you see past their behavior? This can be challenging
sometimes, especially when you do not understand why.

The challenge in developing others is that we see through a
lens of what is present instead of the future. This is why having
a vision for self and the organization is essential. How will you
be able to take others to the promised land if you are unable
to see it? Banerjee says, "The next generation of leadership
will not only be defined by characteristics that are importantly
different from current forms, but will be framed by an entirely
different paradigm that shifts the focus from the "individual as

---

153 Robertson, F. (2015). *The Tale of Two Beasts.* Kane/Miller Publishers.

a leader" to individuals occupying "leadership modalities."[154] For modalities to take place, leaders now have to change their perspective. Do you see people for who they are or what they pretend to be with all the walls, hurt, and disappointments? We need more gold diggers; they will seek the ancient treasures because they know there is value beyond what a regular job would give them. We must move from the traditional models, hierarchy, or centralized management. There has to be an unlocking of people to unlock our organizations. How can we do this if not by changing our perspective?

If we take love with us to work, we will see change. If we speak to an individual's future, we will see change. We will see change if we give grace, knowing no one, not even you, is perfect. If we see our daily work as a service to others, we will see change. If we see people not as machines but as human beings with blood running through their veins, we will see change. We will see change if we do not impose our views on others. Love can only do what we cannot do in our strength. Authentic leadership is grounded in love, which must be issued in service.[155] Love will serve in humility and still have dignity.

When we speak about innovation and strategic foresight for our organizations, grueling work must be done. Explorers who were sent out to find the treasures of the ancient days have yet to have a mindset for a one-day trip back home. They were prepared to remain for months and years, or even die doing a work they believe in. Do you believe in the people? Explorers were willing to die for a cause; their main three goals were *God, Gold, and Glory*. Explorers were innovative leaders; they created new cultures and used different methods to solve problems. There is greatness in all of us. If we want to succeed, we need to be able to see that greatness and be willing to dig for the gold. When gold is discovered, there are unlimited possibilities for everyone to experience. Innovation is not just for the one who discovered

154 Banerjee, Banny. & Ceri, Stefano (eds.). (2016). *Creating Innovation Leaders a Global Perspective. 1st ed.* [Online]. Cham: Springer International Publishing.
155 Engstrom, T. W. (1976). *The making of a Christian leader.* Zondervan.

it; it serves all humanity. Gandhi, Martin Luther King, and Nelson Mandela were all innovative leaders. They went against the traditional ways of going for the gold. Transformational leaders inspire, energize, and intellectually stimulate others.[156] [157]

Live out the golden rule: Treat others as you would treat yourself. Pin this on your wall, mirror, desktop, screen saver, or anywhere you will see it daily: "Love—die for others to Live."

Exercise

Meditate: The gold will appear when I am willing to dig for it.

Observe: Do I see the treasurers in others?

Commit: Dig until I find the gold.

---

156 Banerjee, Banny. & Ceri, Stefano (eds.). (2016). *Creating Innovation Leaders a Global Perspective. 1st ed.* [Online]. Cham: Springer International Publishing.
157 Bass, B. M. (1990, pg 19-31). *From transactional to transformational leadership: Learning to share the vision.* Organizational Dynamics 18(3).

DAY 4

"Outstanding leaders go out of their way to boost the self-esteem of their personnel. If people believe in themselves, it's amazing what they can accomplish."
— **Sam Walton**

We do not need more self-serving, power-hungry leaders; our world has experienced enough of them, and the results are clear. Leaders have been conditioned to think they are to dominate and rule over people. We need leaders who will lead with bravery and selflessness.[158]

Traveling solo can be adventurous, but sailing solo is another spirit of bravery. Jessica Watson, who many of you may know, is a young Australian sailor who set out to travel the world at sixteen years old. The journey took her 23,000 nautical miles and 210 days. Jessica developed a love for sailing from a young age. She started competing at the age of eight. Jessica announced she was going to sail solo around the world in 2009. Many people in the sailing community were against her ambition due to her young age. Jessica asked her parents if they believed she could do it; with their response, she continued with her plans, irrespective of what others thought. Don McIntyre and Tony Mowbray supported Jessica by publicly vouching for her skills and talent. Los Angeles Times reporter Kelly Burgess got a statement from Jessica, "I wanted to challenge myself and achieve something to be proud of. Furthermore, yes, I wanted to inspire people. I hated being judged by my appearance and other people's expectations of what a "little girl" was capable

---

158 Blanchard, K. H. & Broadwell, R. (eds.). (2018). *Servant leadership in action how you can achieve great relationships and results.* Oakland, CA: Berrett-Koehler Publishers, Inc.

of. It is no longer just my dream or voyage. Every milestone out here is not just my achievement but an achievement for everyone who has put so much time and effort into helping get me here."[159]

There were other young sailors under the age of twenty-two, such as Robin Lee Graham, Tania Aebi, Brian Caldwell, David Dicks, Jesse Artin, Zac Sunderland, Michael Perham, and Laura Dekker, who completed a solo trip around the world, some assisted and others unassisted. Either way, these individuals would have never known it was possible if there were no leaders around them speaking about their capabilities. We all have something extraordinary inside of us; the thing that holds us back is fear. Fear will cause stagnation, quitting, complacency, and laziness. Jessica said she used to be a little girl who was scared of everything. She does not remember when the fear left other than her mum's story about her jumping into the pool one day. Jessica said she took the approach of Helen Keller, "If you truly want to live life, you have to get involved."[160] At school, Jessica faced a different type of challenge: dyslexia. Now, she has graduated from college, has written books, does public speaking, and works as a manager.

Blanchard and Broadwell travel around the world teaching about servant leadership and how it can change organizations. They have discovered how organizational leaders want to make the change but need to take the leap of faith. Servant leaders are focused on the greater good of others. The concept of servant leadership is not just for faith-based organizations but for all organizations.[161] Robert Greenleaf coined servant leadership as serving first and leading second.[162]

---

159 Burgess, Kelly. (22 February 2010). *Sailors Abby Sunderland, 16, crosses the equator; Jessica Watson, also 16, nears the southern point of Africa.* Los Angeles Times.
160 Watson, J. (2010). *True Sprit.* Atria
161 Blanchard, K. H. & Broadwell, R. (eds.). (2018). *Servant leadership in action how you can achieve great relationships and results.* Oakland, CA: Berrett-Koehler Publishers, Inc.
162 Greenleaf, R. K. (1977). *Servant leadership: A journey into the nature of legitimate power and greatness.* Paulist Press.

A manager who became the CEO of an organization once said, "It is a life-giving, life-freeing mindset that releases people."[163] When you treat individuals with dignity and respect, you unlock their vast potential. Every leader desires extraordinary talent; here is the kicker: they already have them. They come up with task forces launching new programs to help with retention, and all they need is to rethink how they treat their people. Servant leadership is not managed by the employees; it is about considering them first in every decision. Look at what you value the most, follow the money, and there is the answer.

To serve is to hold, render aid, and provide assistance. To serve, you must be willing to hold up others, even their ladder, if necessary. What would happen if we were to flip the hierarchy with the employees at the top and the leaders at the bottom? Leaders are providing aid for the employees to perform their responsibilities. Employees take responsibility for their roles and show initiative. They feel valued and know how they fit into the organization's bigger picture. Wayne Dyer, the author, shared many times throughout interviews and speeches about having eagles instead of ducks in a pond. He shared that if leaders work for their people as servant leaders, they are helping them become eagles rather than ducks. Ducks waddle around. Eagles soar above the crowds, accomplishing what seemed impossible and making it possible.

Exercise

Meditate: Am I in the business of making ducks or eagles? I can only produce what I am.

Observe: Do employees make decisions without my input? Do they take responsibility or have I placed it all on myself?

Commit: Serve first and lead second.

---

163 Blanchard, K. H. & Broadwell, R. (eds.). (2018).

DAY 5

*"If you're not embarrassed by who you were 12 months ago,
you didn't learn enough."*
— **Alain de Botton**

From the moment we enter this world, we are to grow and develop. Development is inevitable for human beings. We will develop physically and mentally as we go from being a baby to an adult. Babies move from a place of selfishness to selflessness. A selfish person thinks of themselves first in every situation. They are narrow-minded and have a lack of consideration for others. When we look at toddlers, we notice that they do not like to share, and the words "no" and "mine" are at the top of their best-hit list. As we age, cognitive, social, and emotional development should be taking place. At a certain level of cognitive development, inputting new information evolves into the ideas, concepts, and subject "I" truths.[164] Leaders can prevent this from happening if they surround themselves with nothing but yes-people. They will believe a lie before the truth. Watkins says, "One of the biggest challenges organizations face is that changing your mind is some sort of weakness."[165] No matter how smart you are, you can never know everything; even Albert Einstein did not know everything. Many people delude themselves into believing that others cannot perceive their limited understanding. They already know you do not know everything, and when you pretend you do, it undermines your credibility.

Developing others is developing yourself along the way. The relationship between the leader and the follower is a win-win

164 Watkins, A. & Jones, S. (2023). *Lie-ability: How leaders build and break trust.* Abingdon.
165 Watkins, A. & Jones, S. (2023).

for both. Emotional and Social Intelligence (ESI) is the ability to sit with others with opposing views. Not to settle, have tantrums, or walk away from those who disagree with my truths. Remember, your "I" is yours, but we must come to a place where we make it "our" truth. ESI maturity is not typical in business; egos and assertiveness are often thrown around. Developing says others' views can have value and hold some truth. Living the truth is admitting when you are wrong and being willing to change course if necessary. Bob Goff, who has committed to spending his life to save children from modern-day slavery, says, "Leading is about showing and sharing love."[166] Bob has gone as far as placing his cell phone number on the back of his published books. I know you are thinking, "Who would do such a thing, Bob?" He wants people to know he is honest and that they are valued. Leadership begins with love and ends with love.

Leading takes guts, courage, humility, grit, and unwavering faith—that is if you will do it right. Dying daily must take place to lead with respect and not by position. Simply telling people to go over there will not cause them to move. They will move when they see humanity at its weakest and when they are at their strongest. We should be able to grow with one another instead of using aggression to prove our points. Leading without a relationship is dangerous.[167] People will rebel if all they hear are rules and more rules. Guidelines and principles are essential; they are there for safety and efficiency in the process of daily work. Rules without relationships lead to a dead end. Why do customers return to the same stores or use the same services? They have built a relationship with the organization. Success comes down to people and relationships building and growing together. People know when a person has an agenda, so have an agenda with one item: to love them.

---

166 Goff, Bob. (2012). *Love does: Discover a secretly incredible life in an ordinary world.* Thomas Nelson.
167 Gordon, J. (2017). *The power of positive leadership: how and why positive leaders transform teams and organizations and change the world.* Wiley.

Exercise

Meditate: It takes humility to grow.

Observe: Who has opposing views to myself? Do I enjoy speaking with them although it will challenge my intellect?

Commit: Lead with love.

DAY 6

"You grow up the day you have your first real laugh—at yourself."
— **Ethel Barrymore**

Do not take yourself too seriously. We have all heard the saying: Learn to laugh at yourself. It is freeing in comparison to others laughing at you. Earlier philosophers considered laughter to be frivolous. Others saw laughter as a way to release nervous energy. Humans are the only creatures with a sense of humor, which is displayed through laughter.[168] Laughter is displayed when things are comical and amusing. Laughter is an action that comes with a sound. There is a positive psychological shift. Laughter can come from different experiences: jokes, tickling, or a particular act. According to Webster's Dictionary, Amusement is the state or experience, a diversion of the mind from a series of duties.[169] A person can be amused or unamused by a particular experience. The experience can cause the person to laugh, cry, be sad, or be depressed. We have been taught to laugh at individuals' faults and shortcomings, which is why it is difficult to laugh at ourselves. Laughing at others makes people feel superior.

When my husband and I go to a serious event, I prefer to avoid sitting by him. I know it's harsh; he says things that will cause you to burst into laughter, which can distract you. We can be at the theater, recital, movies, church, funeral, game, or a board meeting—you name it—and he will amuse you with

---

168 Morreall, J. (1987). *The philosophy of laughter and humor.* Albany: State University of New York Press.
169 "amusement." 2023. In Merriam-Webster.com. Retrieved December 4, 2023, from https://www.merriam-webster.com/dictionary/amusement

laughter. We have gotten all the comments and looks: "We will kick you out," "How rude," "We paid for these seats, and you are ruining it for us." If looks could kill, I would not be writing this book. Morreall says humor is a social experience.[170] We laugh together alone and socially. Comedians are looking to humor the audience to laughter. Laughter is contentious; it is used for therapy for individuals who are depressed. Have you ever been in a crowd where people were laughing, and you became amused even though you couldn't figure out what they were laughing about? What about when tension is in a space, and someone makes a joke or sends a funny meme or GIF? Humor can reduce stress, and people can get along and live harmoniously.[171] Amusement gets me through a lot of work...and life.

We have to overlook individual flaws and blemishes and laugh when we or they make mistakes.[172] We must first learn to laugh at ourselves before laughing at others. Then, you will know that the laughter comes from a good place. Simon Critchley argues that finding yourself capable of laughing at oneself is finding oneself ridiculous.[173] The superego is put into check; it is no longer the superior master. Sigmund Freud says it promotes the development of healthy relations between the superego and the ego.[174] Laughing at ourselves promotes flexibility and forgiveness and helps us cope better with the incongruities we encounter .[175] Not being able to laugh at our follies means there is a rigidity that we are not willing to let go of. When people cannot let go of their follies, they are not willing to let others do so. The person lacks self-awareness and cannot view the world from multiple perspectives and others' views.[176] Humility comes with

170 Morreall, J (2009, pg 59). *Comic relief: A comprehensive philosophy of humor.* Oxford: Wiley-Blackwell.

171 Gordon, D. (Deborah M.) (2010). *Ant encounters interaction networks and colony behavior (Course Book).* Princeton University Press. https://doi.org/10.1515/9781400835447

172 Erasmus, D. (1941, pg 28). *In praise of folly, trans.* Hoyt Hopewell Hudson. Princeton University Press.

173 Critchley, S. (2002, pg 103). *On humor.* New York: Routledge.

174 Freud, S (1985, pg 433). *Humor in art and literature.* Penguin Books.

175 Gordon, D. (Deborah M.) (2010).

176 Gordon, D. (Deborah M.) (2010). *Ant encounters interaction networks and colony behavior (Course Book).* Princeton University Press. https://doi.org/10.1515/9781400835447

being able to laugh at oneself, which helps foster open-mindedness, patience, and honesty.

I used to be serious about everything. I believed there was a place and time for humor, amusement, and laughter, which was not often. I remember wanting to be free of my thoughts and beliefs about how things should be done. Back then, I smiled a lot, but it was not from a place of humor; instead, it was me being uncomfortable or nervous. The funny thing was that I always thought certain things were amusing but suppressed the thoughts until later in the day when I was alone. One day, out of nowhere, I was at church, and a person was praying, and I just burst out laughing. What they said was funny to me. I could not stop laughing. I had to get up and leave. Whenever I thought about the words and the person, I laughed again the rest of the day. My experience helped me learn to live in the moment and to relax and laugh. I thought about how I prayed or pronounced certain words and laughed. I started having comebacks and witty verbiage for amusement. This helped me not to take myself seriously in the workplace. Giving grace to myself allowed me to give grace to others. Now, you can see me smiling from a mile away because there is something humorous always at play.

Exercise

Meditate: Do not take myself too seriously.

Observe: Am I defensive with others when they attempt to make things lighthearted?

Commit: Laugh a lot at myself and the situations around me.

DAY 7

Take some time today to reflect on the past six days of learning.

- What loads am I willing to share with others?
- Do I allow others to come up with their own solutions, or am I quick to offer advice?
- Am I willing to become an eagle and duplicate my likeness?
- Do I lead with love or through authority?
- When was the last time I laughed at myself?

Developing others is not telling individuals, "Do as I say, not as I do." Leaders must develop themselves first. Development does not start with a position, nor does it end. Development is a lifelong process. As the leader develops, the follower will come along in the process. Have you ever received good information or insight and wanted to share it with others so they can experience the same fulfillment? There is a misconception that the learning and developmental process stops once we become adults. Development only stops when the person decides to stop learning. They no longer engage with others with different viewpoints, backgrounds, cultures, geographical statuses, or perspectives. We should never be like the grumpy older person in the movie who is set in their ways.

The importance of self-development is vital. Followers will develop based on the culture that they are in and the leadership they experience. Followers will model values, identity, emotions, and motives based on their leadership. Leaders can model negative or positive behavior. The negative leader will look to blame others when things go wrong. The positive leader believes people come to work to do a good job. They tell others

"Thank you" regularly for their contributions. Remember the golden rule, "Treat others as you want to be treated." Leaders will go out of their way for others, asking how they can be of service today. Take love with you to work, accept those things that you cannot control, and love those who show up. Have the openness to know that everyone comes to do good work. Affirm them and let them know they are valued. Do not just say it; demonstrate your value for the skills and talents they bring daily. Lastly, love to laugh and do it often. Share in the amusement of one another's mistakes, not of vice, but of virtue. Laughter is good for the soul; it helps reduce stress and anxiety.

Leading is all about them and not about you. Once you are settled in this reality, you are well on your way to developing others.

References

Amusement. (2023). In *Merriam-Webster.com*. Retrieved December 4, 2023, from https://www.merriam-webster.com/dictionary/amusement

Banerjee, B., & Ceri, S. (Eds.). (2016). *Creating Innovation Leaders: A Global Perspective*. Springer International Publishing. https://doi.org/10.1007/978-3-319-28884-3

Bass, B. M. (1990). From transactional to transformational leadership: Learning to share the vision. *Organizational Dynamics, 18*(3), 19–31.

Blanchard, K. H., & Broadwell, R. (Eds.). (2018). *Servant leadership in action: How you can achieve great relationships and results*. Berrett-Koehler Publishers, Inc.

Burgess, K. (2010, February 22). Sailors Abby Sunderland, 16, crosses the equator; Jessica Watson, also 16, nears the southern point of Africa. *Los Angeles Times*. https://www.latimes.com

Chatham, R., & Sutton, B. (2018). *Growing Yourself as a Leader* (1st ed.). BCS Learning & Development Limited.

Critchley, S. (2002). *On humor*. Routledge.

Engstrom, T. W. (1976). *The making of a Christian leader*. Zondervan.

Erasmus, D. (1941). *In praise of folly* (H. H. Hudson, Trans.). Princeton University Press.

Ericsson, K. A., Prietula, M. J., & Cokely, E. T. (2007). The making of an expert. *Harvard Business Review*. Retrieved December 5, 2023, from https://hbr.org/2007/07/the-making-of-an-expert

Fisher, D., Rooke, D., & Torbert, W. R. (2001). *Personal and organizational transformations through action inquiry*. Varsitybooks.com

Freud, S. (1985). *Humor in art and literature*. Penguin Books.

Gardner, W. L., Avolio, B. J., Luthans, F., May, D. R., & Walumbwa, F. (2005). Can you see the real me? A self-based model of authentic leader and follower development. *The Leadership Quarterly, 16*(3), 343–372. https://doi.org/10.1016/j.leaqua.2005.03.003

Garvey Berger, J. (2011). *Changing on the Job: Developing Leaders for a Complex World* (1st ed.). Stanford University Press.

Goff, B. (2012). *Love does: Discover a secretly incredible life in an ordinary world*. Thomas Nelson.

Gordon, D. (2010). *Ant encounters: Interaction networks and colony behavior* (Course Book). Princeton University Press. https://doi.org/10.1515/9781400835447

Gordon, J. (2017). *The power of positive leadership: How and why positive leaders transform teams and organizations and change the world*. Wiley.

Gordon, M. (2010). Learning to laugh at ourselves: Humor, self-transcendence, and the cultivation of moral virtues. *Educational Theory, 60*(6), 735–749.

Greenleaf, R. K. (1977). *Servant leadership: A journey into the nature of legitimate power and greatness*. Paulist Press.

Kegan, R. (1994). *In over our heads: The mental demands of modern life*. Harvard University Press.

Maxwell, J. C. (1998). *The 21 irrefutable laws of leadership: Follow them and people will follow you*. Thomas Nelson.

Morreall, J. (1987). *The philosophy of laughter and humor*. State University of New York Press.

Morreall, J. (2009). *Comic relief: A comprehensive philosophy of humor*. Wiley-Blackwell.

Robertson, F. (2015). *The Tale of Two Beasts*. Kane/Miller Publishers.

Stillman, J. (2023). Researchers finally figured out how long it really takes to form a new habit: The often repeated figure of 21 days turns out to be a myth. *Inc.com*. Retrieved December 7, 2023, from https://www.inc.com/jessica-stillman/researchers-finally-figured-out-how-long-it-really-takes-to-form-a-new-habit.html

Watkins, A., & Jones, S. (2023). *Lie-ability: How leaders build and break trust*. Abingdon.

Watson, J. (2010). *True spirit*. Atria.

Williams, R. (2017). *Black and white: The way I see it*. Atria.

Wilson, E. O., Durlach, N. I., & Roth, L. M. (1958). Chemical releasers of necrophoric behavior in ants. *Psyche, 65*(4), 108–114.

Zenger, J. H., & Stinnett, K. (2010). *The extraordinary coach: How the best leaders help others grow* (1st ed.). McGraw-Hill.

PART 8

WEAVING THE THREADS OF AFFECTION

Love was touched on in previous chapters, but I felt the need to dive deeper into the topic. I believe love can and will change how we lead. Love will change how our organizations operate once we accept its offering of sacrifice. Love is a word that is alive and working around us or through us each day. There is a choice we make daily when it comes to love: embrace it or reject it. It is a word we use lightly but holds the weight of the world. A word that is seen and experienced by deed. Love will:

Chase after you	Be patient with you	Wait on you	Correct you
Be kind to you	Refine you	Comfort you	Listen to you
Show up for you	Shelter you	Protect you	Die for you

Overall, love is foundational for leadership. There is a type of love, in a social or moral sense, that must be present to lead and follow. Love is all things. We cannot live without love. The things we are searching for; we can find in love. The goals we have, we can find in love. The hurt and pain we experience, we can also find love in the darkest moments of life. Often when we think of love, an intimate relationship with a significant other comes to mind. There is more to love than our lustful desires. Love is complex and varies depending on the culture in which we find ourselves. Love is an essential ingredient in the dimensions of human existence and ultimately binds us together with our faith.[177] If we do not exhibit the appropriate amount of love, developing and leading effectively will be damaging.

Love comes in many forms. Love nourishes life into being and makes room for others to flourish.[178] Love is all-encompassing and inclusive. To understand the world and all its colorful fragments, we must learn to accept and practice love. We may be the smartest people on earth and do the most heroic acts, but without love, we are nothing.

---

177 Wirzba, Norman. & Benson, B. E. (2008). *Transforming philosophy and religion love's wisdom.* Bloomington: Indiana University Press.
178 Wirzba, Norman. & Benson, B. E. (2008). *Transforming philosophy and religion love's wisdom.* Bloomington: Indiana University Press.

Why do you think love is important?[179]

The absence of love is behind all serious conflicts.[180] Love is kind and gentle, not harsh and aggressive. Rosenstock-Huessy was a professor who taught in Vermont after being kicked out of Harvard for his daring talks about God. He was supposed to talk about the comparisons of religion, but instead talked about what religion made, how it was made, and why it mattered. He taught passionately and many did not understand his method of delivery. Rosenstock-Huessy believed that the expression of love, hope, and faith welds us through our pain, our responses, our questions and answers, prayers, and dreams.[181] He pointed that we are in search of something that makes human life make sense. He sought after the omnipresence of God. When I looked up the word "love," everything attached was related to some form of religion. When we speak of love, there is no escaping religious beliefs.

To love is to sacrifice. All life depends on sacrifice. Love gives itself away in the most genuine way. The greatest challenge is giving love to people, especially those who have harmed us in some way. In most religions, one of the core values is to remain peaceful with all men. People are not to keep up feuds, as this will only lead to offensive behavior. Love does not celebrate wrongdoing or laugh at other people's mistakes. We all deserve to be loved right where we are, with no judgment. Love shows up in the smallest ways, making the biggest impact.

We can learn a lot by watching children play. I heard about this story from a man who shared how love changed his wife's life. She was a teacher and a young boy came into her class in the middle of the morning. He only had one arm. She was alarmed that the administration did not give her any warning. She was not able to prepare the children. She watched the students' interaction with the new student. She was being care-

---

179 Strand, R. (2009). *Nine Fruits of the Spirits.* New Leaf Press.
180 Rosenstock-Huessy, E. (1966). *The Christian Future or the Mind Outrun.* Harper and Row.
181 Cristaudo, W. (2008). *Power, love and evil contribution to a philosophy of the damaged.* Amsterdam; Rodopi.

ful to make sure everyone behaved appropriately. At the end of the day, she gathered the children up to do an interactive exercise on building community. She told the students to hold their hands up and put both palms together over their heads. As soon as she said it, she remembered the new student. She felt terrible and did not know what to say. One of the students then said, "Chris, we can make our community house together." In that moment, the teacher witnessed the gift of giving love most genuinely. Throughout the day, she had been concerned about how the students were going to behave when she should have been more concerned about how she felt and possible biases toward those with disabilities. Love does not discriminate; it simply loves all of us.

**How do you respond to people
who are different from you?**

DAY 1

"There is no remedy for love but to love more."
— **Henry David Thoreau**

In order to lead effectively, we have to make love a part of who we are and not just view it as a fictional concept. Loving others who have spoken ill about us, been against us, or even harmed us physically can sometimes be a bunch of cow manure, to say the least! Right or wrong, there is justification in the way you feel. The right thing to do is not to inflict pain, but to respond in love, which is easier said than done. We are to love our enemies, not hate them. The only reason we have enemies is that love is not operating in our lives. The person is against me and my cause. I am against their cause. Does this mean we cannot get along? We tend to make things bigger than what they are.

I was not a fighter in the physical sense; my words can light a match. If I ever found myself placing my hands on anyone in a violent way based on anger, I would walk away. I realized walking away was a bigger threat than striking back. There was a story about a young girl who got beaten to death by her "friends" on a trip out of the country. They left her dead in the hotel room. The video was leaked and the girl was not even fighting back while the other girl continually punched her, stomped her, and dragged her until she went unconscious. It was horrific. Love is not violent; hate is violent and evil. When we do not embrace and render love, hate can take root and cause us to do unmentionable acts. In the story, seven families were affected by hate. Everyone lost. The parents whose only child died that day and the parents whose children witnessed and were a part of the hate crime. Hate will cause you to lose each time, but love is victorious.

Who has harmed you in the past, and how can you display love to them?

There are laws in our judicial system, and if violated, they are enforced. Love, however, is a gift without force. When love is violated, it does not retaliate or wound in return. Love is soft, sweet, and tender in all of its fullness. The power of love is power without power—not force, but vulnerability.[182] The law carries a threat, but not love. Love is fearless. Love is not deceived although it believes all and trusts all.[183] Law runs behind, while love runs ahead.[184]

How can we love if we are not willing to trust? That is a big one for me—trust. One day, I reflected on why I could not go without being involved in a certain task. The root issue was trust. I did not trust it would get done, or done right. I was lacking trust in my team members and family. It was hard for me to swallow this pill, but I knew I had to trust. If I desired change in those environments, I would have to trust and love regardless of the outcome. People will not do it your way because they are not you.

"The law prescribes what love has first written. Love without the law is free, but the law without love is blind, harsh, and unbending."[185] Because love is sweet, it anticipates the needs of others and answers before it is asked. Has someone ever provided an answer before you asked for it? Love co-exists with all and finds new ways to create and bind people together. Love affirms and the law tells us no with a threat always looming over our heads. We are to love and honor all men (Romans 12:10).[186]

What action can you take to love all men?

---

182 Wirzba, Norman. & Benson, B. E. (2008). *Transforming philosophy and religion love's wisdom.* Bloomington: Indiana University Press.
183 Derrida, J. (2005). *Rogues: Two Essays on Reason.* Stanford University Press. Xiv.
184 Wirzba, Norman. & Benson, B. E. (2008).
185 Wirzba, Norman. & Benson, B. E. (2008).
186 English Standard version. Bible, 2020.

Exercise

Meditate: Love regardless.

Observation: Do I show the same care toward others who have harmed me?

Commit: Put kindness and forgiveness into action in all situations. Give grace to others and forgive them quickly.

DAY 2

"To love well is the task in all meaningful relationships,
not just romantic bonds."
— **Bell Hooks**

Love belongs in the workplace. When we do not allow love to do its incredible work; we cause more harm than good. Leaders are responsible for the rise and fall of organizations. When an organization has been found mishandling funds, products, people, and resources as a result of an investigation, it leads back to the leadership. Employees are not responsible for setting goals and the strategy of the organization. The Financial Crisis in 2007-2008 was due to leaders. The health industry was fined for taking shortcuts causing the death of patients. Volkswagen cheated on the emission test and falsely rewarded drivers with better mileage. When placed by Congress, the CEO, Michael Horn said, "The actual actions were of a few rogue engineers."[187]

In 2017, United Airlines forced a Vietnamese-Chinese doctor off the plane to allow one of their employees to fly. The doctor refused to get up because he had to be at the hospital for his patients the next day. The supervisor said she did not care and would get the police to escort him off. The incident escalated from there with Dr. Dai being dragged unconsciously off the plane. He suffered injuries to his mouth, teeth, and arm, and suffered a concussion. Witnesses said the incident did not have to escalate and blamed it on the supervisor. They said her tone

---

187 The Independent. (Oct 2015) *Volkswagen emissions scandal.* https://www.independent. co.uk/news/business/news/volkswagen-emissions-scandal-a-few-rogue-engineers-are-to-blame-says-vw-chief-executive-a6687201.html.

was distasteful and aggressive. Dr. Chai remained calm and polite throughout the encounter.[188]

In these examples, we can see how love was not at work and it led to hurt, pain, and mistrust. Trust was hard to build in these economies and organizations based on the outcomes. People were fined and told not to do it again. In Iceland, they took a different approach. In 2018, the Icelandic judiciary sentenced 36 bankers to a total of 93 years in prison.

Iceland's Prime Minister, Bjarni Benediktsson, believed that the nation had lost its trust and needed to heal and reconcile. He saw jailing the bankers "as a necessary part of rebuilding trust and getting to the bottom of what happened."[189] The approach was the right move to make and was an example of how everyone should be held accountable for their actions. Iceland's focus was not on those with money, but on the overall state of its people and what this says about their country and its leaders. Love will hold you accountable. Iceland admitted their mistake and moved forward with a clear set of values.[190] The other organizations apologized, but why was it challenging for the people to believe them? There is a difference between sorry and regret. I believe a lot of them felt regret rather than remorse. Remorse will cause a person to change their behavior. Regret is merely feeling sorry for getting caught and for the shame; it does not bring correction of behavior. People who fall into this way of life believe they are above the judicial system.

Do you believe leaders are responsible first to render love? Why?

In today's workforce, employees are looking to their leaders for clarity, strategic direction, open and honest communication, and financial objectives. They want to feel involved in those

---

188 Wikipedia. *United Express Flight 3411 incident.* https://en.wikipedia.org/wiki/United_Express_Flight_3411_incident
189 Grettisson, V. (Feb 2018). *36 Bankers, 96 Years in Jail.* The Reykjavik Grapevine, 7 https://grapevine.is/news/2018/02/07/36-bankers-96-years-in-jail/.
190 Cox, Marc. (2020). *The business case for love: how companies get bragged about today.* 1st ed. 2020. Cham: Springer International Publishing.

decisions to help move the plan along. The old regime is still operating in "Do As I Say" and expects people to be happy and satisfied. Employees desire meaningful work and to work with others they respect and care about. They do not want to change who they are to become something the corporate world wants. They desire to dress, talk, and conduct themselves in the same manner at home and work.

According to Gallup, 77% of employees worldwide and 69% in the United States of America are not engaged. When employees were surveyed by Gallup and asked about the top three things they would like from their organizations, 48% said they were looking for a better culture and connectivity with their leadership.[191] Why the lack of engagement? Because we still have command and control at play.

The majority of organizations still have middle-aged, old white men who were brought up in the old regime and still follow the same format. They say they want change and are here for both internal and external stakeholders but continue to run operations the same way. The skills needed to create this culture shift are beyond them. They struggle with empathy, are poor listeners, and are head-driven to meet the numbers rather than collaborating to make the numbers work.[192]

Business schools are not listening to businesses or picking up on the trends in statistics of employee engagement. Social skills are needed from leaders. The higher you go, the less technical expertise matters, and the more important soft and emotional skills become. Harvard Business Review highlights the top 10 CEOs of companies, and out of the 10, only one had an MBA. One executive said, "Business students are being taught how to read a financial report but not how to read the room." How to treat others in different cultures is something that can be taught and everyone can benefit. When you are showing love to another person, love does not take into account your personal

191 Gallup. https://www.gallup.com/workplace/229424/employee-engagement.aspx
192 Cox, Marc. (2020). *The business case for love: how companies get bragged about today.* 1st ed. 2020. Cham: Springer International Publishing.

feelings first. Ed Wynn, a comedian, had a saying that he did not yearn to be the wealthiest man in the cemetery.[193] Steve Jobs added to the comic philosophy by saying, "It does not pay to be the wealthiest man in the cemetery if you cannot go to bed at night saying we have done something that matters."[194] Aim to have a clear conscience, knowing that you treated everyone with dignity, respect, and most importantly, love.

How do you lead—by technical knowledge or soft skills?

Exercise

Meditate: Work is relational. Relational is love. I cannot escape it.

Observation: In what ways have I taken responsibility for the relational equity in my organization/team?

Commit: Treat everyone with respect regardless of their role and the way they treat me.

---

193 *Ed Wynn Doesn't Yearn to Be the Wealthiest Man in Cemetery.* 1932 January 19, Boston Globe. Associated Press.
194 Zachary, G. P. and Yamada, K. 25. (May 1993). *"What's Next?: Steve Jobs's Vision, So on Target at Apple, Now Is Falling Short.* Wall Street Journal.

DAY 3

"Love takes off the masks we fear we cannot live without and know we cannot live within."
— James Baldwin

I believe we have been looking at leadership all wrong, which is the reason for the misfires along the way. Leadership is not about leading. Leadership is love. People are drawn by love, not false humility, control, fear, or manipulation. Southwest Airlines is renowned for its exceptional customer service and for being a great place to work. The airline was founded on love and knowing they were doing it not for themselves but for everyone to have an opportunity to travel at a low cost.

Herb Kelleher and Rollin King stayed in litigation for four years to see their dream take flight on June 18, 1971. When it did, it brought Kelleher to tears. Colleen shared a story in *Lead with LUV: A Different Way to Create Real Success* when one of the mechanical engineers died of cancer.[195] Although the airline does not fly bodies, in this case, they decided to send the former employee home to his family in Detroit. They were in a meeting when one of the lead engineers said in 10 minutes the flight was leaving, and they wanted to be excused to go stand by the fence to see the plane take off. Colleen said, "Sure, we all can go." The meeting was adjourned to go stand at the fence in the hot Texas heat. The plane's departure was delayed due to a storm in Houston for forty minutes, but no one moved or complained. Instead, the group of over 100 employees started singing *"Amazing Grace."*

---

195 Blanchard, K. H. & Barrett, C. (2010). *Lead with LUV: a different way to create real success.* 1st edition. Place of publication not identified: FT Press.

This is the kind of love we bring to work with us every day at Southwest. The organization's culture prioritizes employees first and customers second. When employees are brought onboard to Southwest, they are shown a pyramid with three tiers at the top. They are told they are the most important people to the company and are their number one priority. Southwest leaders will spend 80% of the time treating their employees with the *Golden Rule* and making sure they have an enjoyable work environment and a place where they feel good about themselves, what they do, and their position in the organization. If they do their 80%, Southwest expects the employees to consistently treat the customers with the same respect and care in return. This approach gives the organization returning customers and the best marketing tool—word of mouth. The organization will make money, secure jobs, and please its third tier of customers and shareholders. It is a win-win for everybody.

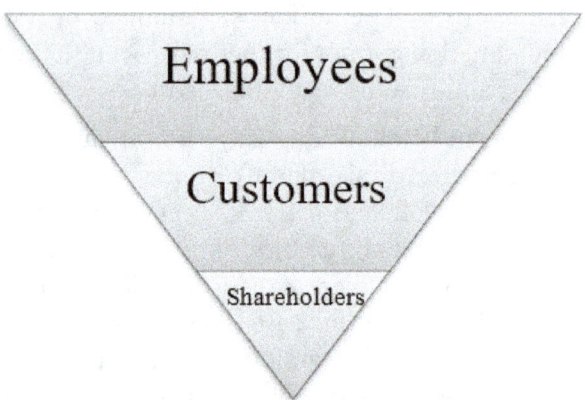

Are you able to flip the pyramid and put the employees at the top? How would this look in your organization?

Organizational culture starts with leadership. The vision, values, and direction will develop the culture. How we view one another, our customers, our mission, and our values will all dictate the culture. If leaders are not willing to go the distance for others, it's time to take a second look at their values and vision.

A famous magician was sharing his story of losing his father when he was one year old. He and his brother were told about it by their mother when he was eight years old. His father, Mr. Z, owned a restaurant. Mr. Z and a server named Ralph were closing up and they noticed three young men approaching. Mr. Z told Ralph to go back inside. The three young boys shot Mr. Z six times in the chest; it was a gang initiation. The server believed the owner knew they were in danger and made a choice to give up himself for another. Ralph experienced unwavering love that night. Both men had wives and children. The leader chose to go the distance. Ralph is a grandfather and the three young boys are now men sitting in prison.

The famous magician has compassion for the men who were once boys. He says, "They probably did not have fathers themselves and turned to a place that was providing them a sense of belonging at the time. Those boys are different now." I wonder about the vision of the restaurant. I am certain they valued their employees first. When organizations say they value the employees first, are they willing to be the sacrificial lamb? This is a question that we have to ask ourselves and be honest about where we are in valuing people.

The Armed Forces are not the only ones dealing with the enemy infiltrating our ranks. Terrorist attacks are real. Active shooters are real. Racism is real. Envy is real. Jealousy is real. We do not know what each day will bring. We hope that when we go to our places of work, whether virtual or in-person, we leave better than when we showed up.

Love will serve. Love is bottom-up. Those at the bottom are serving those at the top. If our organizations are structured with the traditional hierarchy of top-down leadership, our people are not the priority; I am the priority—my name, who I am, is the value. The reason why people are not staying for the long haul is that they are in high pursuit of value. My husband told me the other day, "I do not care about a raise. I am more concerned about what works best for me in this season of my life—not being away from home for long periods of time, driving in traffic for extended periods of time, and people valuing the skills I bring to the organization."

Leaders can say all they want, but the culture speaks for itself. Leaders serve and are responsible for people's needs, training, and development that will let them soar like eagles.[196] Employees are focused on meeting the needs of the leaders. They are too tired to meet the needs of customers 100 percent of the time.

Southwest leadership believes that human satisfaction for employees and customers comes from providing employees with the power and authority to make decisions as long as they are not illegal, unethical, or immoral.[197] Allow people to be the eagles they are, and get them out of the pond that leads nowhere.

What are you willing to sacrifice to lead?

Exercise

Meditate: Love is bottom-up. Leaders are the foundation of their teams and organizations.

Observation: What sacrifices have I made and am willing to make?

Commit: Flip the pyramid to meet the needs of the employees.

---

196 Blanchard, K. H. & Barrett, C. (2010). *Lead with LUV: a different way to create real success. 1st edition.* Place of publication not identified: FT Press.
197 Blanchard, K. H. & Barrett, C. (2010).

DAY 4

"Love is patient, love is kind. It does not envy, it does not boast, it is not proud. It does not dishonor others, it is not self-seeking, it is not easily angered, it keeps no record of wrongs. Love does not delight in evil but rejoices with the truth. It always protects, always trusts, always hopes, always perseveres."
— 1 Corinthians 13:4-7

Whether you believe in Jesus as your savior or not, the principle of love stands true no matter your beliefs. The success of an organization or an individual falls on the principles mentioned in 1 Corinthians 13: 4-7.[198]

The New International	The Message
Love is patient.	Love never gives up.
Love is kind.	Love cares more for others than for self.
It does not envy,	Love doesn't want what it doesn't have.
It does not boast,	Love doesn't strut,
It is not proud,	Doesn't have a swelled head,
It does not dishonor others.	Doesn't force itself on others,
It is not self-seeking,	Isn't always "me first,"
It is not easily angered,	Doesn't fly off the handle,
It keeps no record of wrongs.	Doesn't keep score of the sins of others,
Love does not delight in evil but rejoices with the truth.	Doesn't revel when others grovel, Takes pleasure in the flowering of truth,
It always protects,	Puts up with anything,
Always trusts,	Trusts God always,
Always hopes,	Always looks for the best,
Always perseveres.	Never looks back,
Love never fails.	But keeps going to the end.

Whether we want to believe that love belongs in the workplace or not, you can see how the list equates to valuing one another. How

198 English Standard version. Bible, 2020.

can you expect people to trust you if you are not kind and patient with them? How can you get people to do their best work if you hold their mistakes against them? How can you get people to see their potential if you cannot see the best in them? Love is selfless.

We are not perfect human beings, and we struggle in different ways. The goal is not perfection. We should aim for acceptance. Once I have accepted this is where I fall, I can start to do better. I struggled with staying humble and finding the balance of knowing my power and that it never belonged to me. Taking credit for work I had done or ideas that I contributed would frustrate me. Fred Smith, author of *You and Your Network*, said, "People with humility don't deny their power; they just recognize that it passes through them, not from them."[199]

I had to change my view and my value system. Was it for me or others? There are fifteen items on the *Love List*, and I demonstrate each one, struggling with some more than others. The great thing is that I recognize how I may or may not be operating in love. Each day that I am alive, I strive to become a living, breathing embodiment of love; it will take dying, and I am willing to die to live. If you want to lead with the principles of love and see your team or organization thrive, go through the list and see when you demonstrated each one.

Have you struggled in leading with love? In what areas?

Exercise

Meditate: Love values one another.

Observation: Do I display the 15 action items on what love must do in 1 Corinthians 13?

Commit: In the areas where the answer to the previous question was no, be intentional about taking action with others in those areas.

---

199 Smith, F. (1998). *You and Your Network*. Executive Books.

DAY 5

"Continue to share your heart with people even if it has been broken."
— **Amy Poehler**

As we get to a closing point on the topic of love, let's address the opposite of love—fear. Yes, fear will keep you from doing what you know to be right. I am not perfect. There is no perfect human being. Yet, we often act as if there is this level of perfection everyone must reach. I have done damage to teams I have led by operating in fear and this untenable goal of perfection that I placed on myself and, in turn, on others.

Those fears were those of self-doubt, imperfection, and failure. Fear does not work; it causes people to draw away instead of being unified. Fear will influence your actions in how you treat others and how you live, both personally and professionally.[200]

Fear originates in our minds and then triggers a physical response in our bodies. The amygdala, a small organ in the middle of the brain, sends an alert to our nervous system. When we are scared, molecules of glutamate (a neurotransmitter) travel to the hypothalamus. This then triggers the autonomic nervous system and produces a response that you can't control.[201] Adrenaline and cortisol are released and the body goes into motion. Blood flows away from your heart into your limbs, making it easier to either run or fight.

---

200 Bryant, J. (2009). *Love leadership the new way to lead in a fear-based world. 1st ed.* San Francisco: Jossey-Bass.
201 Adolphs, R. (2013). *The Biology of Fear.* Curr Biol. 2013 Jan 21; 23(2): R79–R93. doi: 10.1016/j.cub.2012.11.055.

It takes no work or effort to experience fear. However, love comes from the part of the brain that thinks, remembers, and finds meaning in life. Love is feeling plus thought.[202] Love survives while fear dies. Bill Clinton shared with Bryant how fear can hold a person back: "People fear failure, inadequacy, rejection, a recurrence of past hurts for themselves or loved ones, and the unknown. No one is immune to some or all of these fears. That's why real living takes courage—to act, grow, change, and get up and try again and again."

Some scholars believe that fear can play a productive role in organizations. "Fear can motivate behavior if employees perceive that they can cope with the resulting threat."[203]

Those who are under pressure will either fight or fly. The majority take flight, and those who fight are sometimes fighting the wrong opponent. When we become stuck in our train of thought of how something should be done, we are fighting ourselves and our customers. There is no victory for the organization in the end.

Love is both inward and outward and starts with oneself. We all need to know our True North to be our authentic selves.[204] As leaders who are raising other leaders, we pass on bad habits and fear. We do not know how to do better when we do know that we need to do better. We are not the be-all in this world or even in our organization. There will always be someone smarter. Do not kick them out. Fear suggests they will take your job, but even if they do, does it matter? Something is waiting for you, so embrace them in love and draw out from the well, so you can be better.

Ultimately, each of us has to decide what type of leader we want to be and what kind of leadership we want the future

---

202 Bryant, J. (2009). *Love leadership the new way to lead in a fear-based world. 1st ed.* San Francisco: Jossey-Bass.
203 Kinni, T. (Oct 2020). *The fear factor: In the right circumstances, fear can be a powerful motivating force.* https://www.strategy-business.com/blog/The-fear-factor.
204 George, B., William W., Sims, P., & Sims, P., Peter E. (2007). *True north discover your authentic leadership (1st. ed.).* Jossey-Bass.

world to experience. Do you want others to experience fear as you might have, or love? In the early 2000s, renowned film producer Scott Rudin held the title of the "most feared boss." Rudin would throw things at assistants, and he had over 250 in five years.[205] People did not know what to expect when they came to work. They were fearful of him and their livelihood. His films are famous and made a lot of money, but at what cost?

Fear can make you think that money and power will eliminate all problems. Remember, everything we do in life goes through a person. One global study involving 220,000 employees highlighted the widespread phenomenon of bullying and harassment at work.[206] High rates of bullying were reported in South America, the Asia–Pacific, and Middle Asia regions. In North America (Canada, the Caribbean, Mexico, and the United States of America), it was found that 63 percent of employees have experienced workplace bullying.

In another study, 58 percent of bullies were superiors, 26 percent were peers, 43 percent were subordinates, and some were from other unknown areas.[207]

According to Bryant, fear-based leadership tactics are:

- Using aggressive language, tone, and eye contact
- Criticizing unfairly
- Blaming, without offering reasonable recourse
- Applying rules inconsistently
- Stealing credit
- Making unreasonable demands
- Issuing threats, insults, and accusations
- Denying accomplishments

205 Kelly, K. and Marr, M., *"Boss-Zilla!"* Wall Street Journal, September 24, 2005, http://online.wsj.com/article/SB112749746571150033.html.
206 León-Pérez, J. M., Escartín, J., & Giorgi, G. (2021, pg 55-86). *The presence of workplace bullying and harassment worldwide.* Concepts, approaches, and methods.
207 Djurkovic, N., McCormack, D., & Casimir, G. (2008). *Workplace bullying and intention to leave: The moderating effect of perceived organizational support.* Human Resource.Management Journal, 18(4), 405–422. https://doi.org/10.1111/j.1748-8583.2008.00081.x.

- Excluding others from opportunities
- Assigning pointless tasks
- Personalizing problems
- Breaching confidentiality
- Spreading rumors

Leading with fear is not sustainable, and it damages relationships and organizations. Niccolò Machiavelli, in his work "The Prince," once asked whether leaders should be loved or feared. He told his court that one would like to be both, but if one must choose, then choose fear.[208]

Men are ungrateful, inconsistent, feigners, dissimulators, avoiders of danger, eager for gain, and out for themselves. Love is held by chains. Fear is held by punishment, and it will desert you. The state of our countries can attest to Machiavelli being wrong. Look at leaders who led with light and the ones who led with darkness. How did it turn out?

John Hope Bryant, the founder of Operation HOPE, shared a time when he mobilized every known resource to build a cyber cafe for the vice president's visit within two weeks. They pulled it off, but John had a moment of fear and placed it on those who were working alongside him. He jumped on his desk and yelled at those who were around because the printer was not working.

A mentor and 15-year volunteer named Rod witnessed the behavior. He told him, "I am going to forgive because all of this is stressful, but do not let it happen again. Now what do you need me to do?" Bryant said he learned a great lesson that day. Fear had him. But those calm words of love allowed fear to break off. Rod was loving and gracious. John made a promise never to let fear control him. He would take his fears and push through them with dignity.

---

208 Machiavelli, N. (1995). *The Prince and Other Political Writings, trans.* Stephen J. Milner Everyman Paperbacks.

Rod taught him that when you have power, you do not need to use it. John learned to talk without being offensive, to listen without being defensive, and to leave even his adversaries with their dignity intact. He would learn to love those he did not like. He would love those who did not deserve love in return. Then, and only then, would he be totally free.[209]

Exercise

Meditate: Love is not FEAR.

Observation: Do I give love or fear to team members?

Commit: Do not abuse my power and authority. Share it with those I am in community with.

209 Bryant, J. (2009). *Love leadership the new way to lead in a fear-based world. 1st ed.* San Francisco: Jossey-Bass.

DAY 6

"Love is given without a requirement."
— **Reneé Murdock**

Organizations are not complete without love. Love and business do go hand in hand. We are human beings who desire love and acceptance. Love is meant for every facet of life. Human behavior is often motivated by one or more of the types of love:[210] family (storge), friendly (philia), romantic (eros), self-love (philautia), hospitality (xenia), and unconditional (agape).

We tend to pick and choose which love we want to give, and most would give philia, a friendly love toward those in the workplace. While this is good, philia lacks the key element in transformational leading and living—unconditional love. Philia says we are good until we are not good. For instance, you did not agree with my idea. Then, you cut me off while I was speaking, you did not complete your part of the project, or you did not show up.

Agape says no matter what you do, I am going to love you right where you are because no one is perfect. Organizations are fearful of using the word love, and they do not want to be seen as not taking care of their employees. Who wants to be listed in the top 50 places not to work? Agape changes how we interact with one another and how our organizations flourish.

Authentic, servanthood and transformational leadership theories involve serving, respecting others, exemplifying honesty,

---

210 Hummels, H., Lee, M. T., Nullens, P., Ruffini, R., & Hancock, J. (2021, pg 329-353). *The Future on Love and Business Organizing An Agenda for Growth and Affirmation of People and the Environment (AGAPE).* Humanistic Management Journal, 6(3),. https://doi.org/10.1007/s41463-021-00117-x.

being fair, and building healthy communities.[211] Leaders should avoid using people or manipulating them to get what they want, leaving them to fend for themselves. Instead, they should generate positive psychological capital in the workplace, increasing efficacy, optimism, and resiliency.[212]

Love embraces ethics and morality. It is not a private issue, but a public one. How we treat employees, customers, stakeholders, and our communities is all public. We want to make everyone aware of what we stand for and how we are going to get it done. There is a moral duty to share our vision and mission statements with the public. In a religious format, people are taught to love their neighbors. Does this apply in secular workplaces? Yes! We cannot escape work or others. We live with others and should love them as we love ourselves.

Scholarly research shows that when individuals are shown love, there is less turnover, higher levels of employment satisfaction, trust among coworkers, and a secure work environment.[213]

Immanuel Kant was a German philosopher during the Enlightenment era. The majority of his beliefs were based on his religious views. He stated, "I had to deny knowledge in order to make room for faith." He believed that neighborly love is an act of readiness to promote the happiness of others, although he believed in racism, slavery, and segregation until the last decade of his life. Kant also believed that love cannot be commanded, saying, "Love is a matter of feeling, not of willing, and I cannot love because I will to, still less because I ought to, I cannot be constrained to love."[214] He says there is a moral obligation for practical love.

---

211 Northouse, P. G. (2019). *Leadership: Theory and Practice (Eighth ed.).* SAGE.

212 Luthans, F., C.M. Youssef-Morgan, and B.J. Avolio. (2015). *Psychological Capital and Beyond (Har/Psc edition).* Oxford University Press.

213 Barsade, S. G., & O'Neill, O. A. (2014, pg 551-598). *What's love got to do with it? A longitudinal study of the culture of companionate love and employee and client outcomes in a long-term care setting.* Administrative Science Quarterly, 59(4).

214 Kant, I. (1797/2017). *The metaphysics of morals. Cambridge texts in the history of philosophy* (M. Gregor, & J. Timmermann, Eds.). Cambridge University Press

LEADERSHIP EVOLUTION

Unconditional love will transform how we do business with one another. Unconditional means unlimited, unreserved, un-questioning, unqualified, and unrestricted. There are no strings attached to this love. In the other types of love, there are condi-tions placed on the level of love someone is willing to give.

A humanistic psychologist named Carl Rogers believed an individual needed an environment that provides genuineness, acceptance, empathy, and approval.[215] A healthy loving envi-ronment is where change happens.

Abraham Maslow said that for people to grow, they had to have a positive perspective on themselves.[216] Human beings do not start off loving one another because we are naturally self-centered beings. We learn how to love; this is the ultimate goal. Learning to love involves accepting love first and being intentional in giving, not like suggested by Kant, with restraints, but with pure freedom.

Love is transformational; it changes how we see the world. If you had access to something with no monetary cost that could lead to you having a thriving organization, wouldn't you want to go for it? Love is right here waiting with open arms and it is not leaving, whether you embrace it today or ten years from now.

Exercise

Meditate: Love has no requirements.

Observation: Am I afraid to say the words "I love you" to coworkers? Am I afraid to express agape love?

Commit: Change how my team works, and express my love for them by showing up each day, when they get it right, and most importantly, when they get it wrong.

---

215 Rogers, C. (1973, pg 176-189). *The Interpersonal Relationship: The Core of Guidance.* In, Raymond M. Maslowski, Lewis B. Morgan (Eds.), Interpersonal Growth and Self Actualization in Groups.
216 Maslow, A. H. (1961, pg 254-260). *Peak Experiences as Acute Identity Experiences.* Am. J. Psychoanal. 21 (2). doi:10.1007/bf01873126. S2CID 144166139.

DAY 7

Love does not come with constraints. It is not fear, demanding, commanding, or rude. Love is patience, gentleness, and kindness. We can do a lot of things in the world, but there is nothing greater than to love others. Love belongs in every area of our lives, not only in family or significant others. You can take love to work and express the fullness of how it transforms the lives of others. Take some time today to reflect on the following questions when it comes to love and leading in today's organizations.

- Who has harmed you in the past; how can you display love to them?

- Do you believe leaders are responsible first to render love? Why?

- Have you struggled in leading with love? In what areas?

- What are you willing to sacrifice to lead?

- What action can you take to love all people?

Loving others is a choice you can make if you don't allow fear to keep you bound like a duck. Allow love to set you free like an eagle. Great leadership is leadership that leads with love. The choice to develop as a leader is one that takes initial actions daily. How we treat ourselves is a reflection of how we will treat others. I encourage you to be kind and gracious to yourself and show the same manner toward others. Becoming does not happen overnight. Each day, as you rise, remember that there is a new opportunity to learn and grow.

May you find joy and peace on your journey to becoming.

References

Adolphs, R. (2013). The biology of fear. *Current Biology*, 23(2), R79–R93. https://doi.org/10.1016/j.cub.2012.11.055

Barsade, S. G., & O'Neill, O. A. (2014). What's love got to do with it? A longitudinal study of the culture of companionate love and employee and client outcomes in a long-term care setting. *Administrative Science Quarterly*, 59(4), 551–598.

Blanchard, K. H., & Barrett, C. (2010). *Lead with LUV: A different way to create real success* (1st ed.). FT Press.

Bryant, J. (2009). *Love leadership: The new way to lead in a fear-based world* (1st ed.). Jossey-Bass.

Cox, M. (2020). *The business case for love: How companies get bragged about today* (1st ed.). Springer International Publishing.

Cristaudo, W. (2008). *Power, love and evil: Contribution to a philosophy of the damaged*. Rodopi.

Derrida, J. (2005). *Rogues: Two essays on reason*. Stanford University Press.

Djurkovic, N., McCormack, D., & Casimir, G. (2008). Workplace bullying and intention to leave: The moderating effect of perceived organisational support. *Human Resource Management Journal*, 18(4), 405–422. https://doi.org/10.1111/j.1748-8583.2008.00081.x

Ed Wynn Doesn't Yearn to Be the Wealthiest Man in Cemetery. (1932, January 19). *Boston Globe*. Associated Press, p. 12.

English Standard Version. (2020). *Bible*.

Gallup. (n.d.). https://www.gallup.com/workplace/229424/employee-engagement.aspx

George, B., Sims, P., & Sims, P. (2007). *True north: Discover your authentic leadership* (1st ed.). Jossey-Bass.

Grettisson, V. (2018, February 7). 36 bankers, 96 years in jail. *The Reykjavik Grapevine*. https://grapevine.is/news/2018/02/07/36-bankers-96-years-in-jail/

Hummels, H., Lee, M. T., Nullens, P., Ruffini, R., & Hancock, J. (2021). The future on love and business organizing: An agenda for growth and affirmation of people and the environment (AGAPE). *Humanistic Management Journal*, 6(3), 329–353. https://doi.org/10.1007/s41463-021-00117-x

Japan Inc.: A corporate culture on trial after scandals. (2018, January 3). *The Financial Times*. https://www.ft.com/content/26d4843a-e743-11e7-97e2-916d4fbac0da

Kant, I. (2017). *The metaphysics of morals* (M. Gregor & J. Timmermann, Eds.). Cambridge University Press. (Original work published 1797)

Kelly, K., & Marr, M. (2005, September 24). Boss-Zilla! *Wall Street Journal*. http://online.wsj.com/article/SB112749746571150033.html

Kinni, T. (2020, October 29). The fear factor: In the right circumstances, fear can be a powerful motivating force. *Strategy+Business*. https://www.strategy-business.com/blog/The-fear-factor

León-Pérez, J. M., Escartín, J., & Giorgi, G. (2021). The presence of workplace bullying and harassment worldwide. In *Concepts, approaches and methods* (pp. 55–86).

Luthans, F., Youssef-Morgan, C. M., & Avolio, B. J. (2015). *Psychological capital and beyond* (Har/Psc ed.). Oxford University Press.

Machiavelli, N. (1995). *The prince and other political writings* (S. J. Milner, Trans.). Everyman Paperbacks.

Maslow, A. H. (1961). Peak experiences as acute identity experiences. *American Journal of Psychoanalysis*, 21(2), 254–260. https://doi.org/10.1007/bf01873126

Northouse, P. G. (2019). *Leadership: Theory and practice* (8th ed.). SAGE.

Rogers, C. (1973). The interpersonal relationship: The core of guidance. In R. M. Maslowski & L. B. Morgan (Eds.), *Interpersonal growth and self-actualization in groups* (pp. 176–189).

Rosenstock-Huessy, E. (1966). *The Christian future or the mind outrun*. Harper and Row.

Smith, F. (1998). *You and your network*. Executive Books.

Strand, R. (2009). *Nine fruits of the spirit*. New Leaf Press.

Volkswagen emissions scandal. (2015, October 9). *The Independent*. https://www.independent.co.uk/news/business/news/volkswagen-emissions-scandal-a-few-rogue-engineers-are-to-blame-says-vw-chief-executive-a6687201.html

Wikipedia. (n.d.). United Express Flight 3411 incident. https://en.wikipedia.org/wiki/United_Express_Flight_3411_incident

Wirzba, N., & Benson, B. E. (2008). *Transforming philosophy and religion: Love's wisdom*. Indiana University Press.

Zachary, G. P., & Yamada, K. (1993, May 25). What's next?: Steve Jobs's vision, so on target at Apple, now is falling short. *Wall Street Journal*.

SUMMARY

Painting the Portrait of Integrity

Answer the following questions:

- Who am I?

- Do my actions align with my words?

- What are others saying about me, both privately and publicly?

Your character defines who you are, and it will speak before you show up and when you leave. Character is the foundation of leadership: integrity, humility, accountability, and courage. People who examine themselves daily know why they do what they do. Your posture starts from the heart and everything flows from it.

Meditate

- There is a price for leading.

- Healing starts by forgiving myself first.

- True honor is holding to what is honest and right.

- What is lovely and what is true?

- Leadership is not about being given authority; it has to be earned by putting yourself out there.

Mirror, Mirror

Answer the following questions:

- What things have I walked past without giving consideration?

- Who am I comparing myself to and why?

- What happens when I get upset or disagree? How does my body respond? How do others respond?

- When I make a mistake, what is my response? Do I take responsibility or blame others? When others make a mistake, what is my response?

People increasingly engage with machines rather than each other, spending an average of 8 hours daily on screens, with 2 hours dedicated to social media. Developing self-awareness can elevate your leadership skills, strengthen relationships, and positively influence your team and organization. Influential leaders have high Emotional Intelligence (EI). Emotional Intelligence comprises five components: self-awareness, self-regulation, self-motivation, social skills, and empathy. Self-awareness is being aware of one's psychological state at all times. You cannot be afraid to express your emotions.

Meditate

- Beautiful things that cannot be seen or touched.

- Comparing myself to others is not wise; it will only lead to envy and jealousy.

- Look within to find the true me.

- There are areas that I have ignored, and they are underdeveloped.

- Mistakes are bound to happen. Am I making the same ones?

- Do not ignore those blocked spaces; expose and address them.

Shining Light on Shadows

Answer the following questions:

- What is my response when others point out how I address or do not address a situation?

- How do I respond when others tell me the idea will not work?

- How do I listen to others?

- How much do I search for truth?

- How is my heart? What changes have I made?

There is a spot in our retina where the optic nerve connects. In these areas, there are no light-sensitive cells; this is called the "blind spot." We all have them and there is no escaping it. Being aware of what they are is imperative in how you will lead. Blind spots affect our decision-making. When we can only see what is right in front of us, we must depend on others to bring awareness of what is not visible. When you know better, you should do better. Listening to others about what they see, and challenging what you believe about yourself is crucial for personal and professional growth.

Meditate

- I have blind spots; I must be intentional about closing the gap.

- The world is a wonder, and I am unable to see it all from where I sit.

- My model of what is reality is not complete.

- Not all information is factual. It is information, and I should continue to seek out the truth.

- What I am willing to learn, I am able to see.

- Change starts with me as a leader.

Follow the leader

Answer the following questions:

- How do I respond to authority?

- How do I use my authority? Is it in an ethical way?

- Am I selfish or selfless?

- Are team members coming to speak with me openly and honestly about how they feel about the direction the organization is going?

- How do I respond when I am approached with conflict or questioned about my decisions?

- Do people speak out in meetings? How do I respond to their comments?

Let me break through the myth. Following is not a weakness. If you think about it, everyone is following willingly or unwillingly in life. I personally would rather be on the willing side. To lead, you must first follow. Following takes as much courage as leading. Leaders can push followers and followers can push their leaders. They are interchangeable, and one needs the other. There are five types of followers according to Riggo (Riggo, 2008): the sheep, yes-people, the alienated, the pragmatics, and the stars. It is important to know what type of follower you and those on your team are. Knowing who to assign and pairing team members properly can help expedite initiatives.

Meditate

- A good follower is a good leader.

- If I am a leader, I am a follower.

- Follow the FOLLOWER.

- Loyalty does not mean always agreeing with me.

- Constructive criticism and conflict are not negative.

- A one-man team will never accomplish all it was set out to do.

- Relationships are important.

Heartstrings and Handshakes

Answer the following questions:

- Do I only reach out to my team members when I need something? Do I genuinely care about their well-being and growth?

- How do I listen to others? What new things do I learn daily? And from whom?

- What strengths and weaknesses do I see in each team member?

- How does each person in my team show up? How do they respond to one another? How do they acknowledge one another's emotions?

- Who am I lifting up each day? Am I aware of any unethical issues that I have not addressed?

- How am I vulnerable?

The art of a relationship is how two or more concepts, objects, or people are connected, or the state of being connected. There is a bond that forms, guiding these concepts in a particular direction. As leaders, it is important to come together with followers, not just in a professional way, but also on a personal level. You spend most of your waking hours with the people you work with, not your family. In Western culture, we see relationships as transactional and wonder what we can get from the other person. Asian culture views relationships as vital to business success. They look for connections and common ground. If there are problems in the family or organization, they evaluate their relationships. Heifetz & Linsky say the most important thing between two human beings is connection.

Meditate

- Relationships and friendships require intentional work.
- Curiosity creates learning.

- I am a small piece of the bigger picture.
- All skills are valuable for everyone.
- I am a city that sits on a hill for all to see.
- Leadership is relational.

Work Worth Doing

Answer the following questions:

- How do I show up to work? Are people running from me or toward me? Am I complaining or appreciative?
- Do I love what I do?
- What work feeds my heart?
- Do I know my values?
- What drives my life?
- Does my vision align with the organization?

The answers to these questions provide a clear view of how you view work. Are you waiting idly, dreading to clock in and make the donuts each day? When you do what you love, it is not work. It is a service of love to others. You will never get away from work, even when you believe you are retired.

You may grow tired of doing what you were doing and seek new ventures. However, statistics show that individuals who are active live longer than those who are not actively engaged daily. My husband's grandmother gets up in the morning and reads her Bible. Twice a week, she goes to "work" (she volunteers). The other days, she is at meetings, luncheons, funerals, or church. When she calls you back, she will say, "Grandma was at work." Grandma still drives, takes no medicine, cooks for herself, and cleans, all at the prime age of 92. If Grandma is still working in joy, so can you.

When people want to leave, send them off with a blessing. When you see it is time for someone to go, send them off with a blessing. We have to change our perspectives when it comes to work and realize we were all created to do different things at different times throughout life. Your work is a service to others. Can you imagine how our world would be if everyone stopped working?

Meditate

- I cannot control the world. I can control my attitude and work ethic.

- There is purpose, passion, creativity, and love in me.

- The meaningfulness of work is what I believe to be meaningful.

- I need to find my voice so that it aligns with my words and deeds.

- My role is not my identity.

- For great workplaces to exist, I have to bring value, trust, and love to work.

Growing Together

Answer the following questions:

- How many people from my team can I leave in charge and not be concerned about target dates being missed?

- Do I listen and ask a lot of questions? Do I offer up advice to quickly to get to the next thing? Does the conversation shut down?

- Do I see the treasures in others?

- Do employees make decisions without my input? Do they take responsibility, or have I placed it all on myself?

- Who has opposing views to mine? Do I enjoy speaking with them even though it will challenge my intellect?

- Am I defensive with others when they attempt to make things lighthearted?

Leaders model development. They must grow to help others grow. "Do as I say, not as I do" is not going to work in developing others. Followers will model values, identity, emotions, and motives based on their leadership. How leaders are developed can impact the culture of organizations. John Maxwell says we should look at the development process like investing in the stock market: "Success is not going to happen overnight." People spend years growing their wealth. Look at development through the same lens. You have to be in it for the long game.

Meditate

- I am not built to carry the load alone.

- Solving someone else's problem is a roadblock to their discovery of a resolution.

- The gold will appear when I am willing to dig for it.

- Am I in the business of making ducks or eagles? I can only produce what I am.

- It takes humility to grow.

- I should never take myself too seriously.

Weaving the Threads of Affection

Answer the following questions:

- Do I show the same care toward others who have harmed me?

- In what ways have I taken responsibility for the relational equity in my organization/team?

- What sacrifices have I made to lead, and what am I willing to make?

- Do I display the 15 action items on what love must do in 1 Corinthians 13?

- Do I give love or fear to team members?

- Am I afraid to say the words "I love you" to coworkers? Are you afraid to express agape love?

Love covers and changes all things. Where there is fear, there is no love. Love is patient. Love is kind. It does not envy, it does not boast it is not proud, it does not dishonor others. Love is not self-seeking, it is not easily angered, it keeps no record of wrongs. Love does not delight in evil but rejoices with the truth. It always protects, always trusts, always hopes, and always perseveres. Love never fails. Who would not want to experience love at work? Love belongs in the workplace and not just with family and close friends. Love is the foundation of leadership. When you are leading effectively, love is holding you up. Love is complex and has many variances to it depending on the cultures in which we find ourselves. Love is an essential ingredient in the dimensions of human existence and ultimately binds us together and our faith (Wirzba & Benson, 2008).

Meditate

- Love regardless.

- Work is relational. Relational is love. You cannot escape it.

- Love is bottom-up. Leaders are the foundation of their teams and organizations.

- Love values one another.

- Love is not FEAR.

- Love has no requirements.

CONCLUSION

You made it! I hope that you have been fulfilled in numerous ways on this journey. The journey of becoming is less traveled. The path is not as clear as others because you have to clear the path yourself. Becoming is individual soul work. Working on the soul will cause a transformation. The way you used to think, behave, and see the world is completely different. People will think you have gone astray and might even want to disconnect. I want you to know that it is okay. New connections and even old connections will become richer.

Our organizations are suffering, not because of government leaders or the economy. We leaders are the cause, and as soon as we confess, we can start to turn things around. The change has to start with the leaders. How you lead determines how the organization responds to external and internal challenges. As you have worked on your soul in these 56 days, do not stop here. Becoming is a daily work until the day you leave the Earth. There will always seem as though something is missing because once you find it, there will be something else. This is how we grow into the fullness of our potential in leadership.

I challenge you to keep meditating on the key elements of Leadership: Character, Self-Awareness, Blind Spots, Followership, Relationships, Working, Developing Others, and Love. They will help in the continual growth process. Leaders are made, not born. Effective leaders worked on themselves to better serve others. Their service and heart toward others are what made them effective. The position, title, and economic status, did not matter; they understood their assignment and did not abuse power and authority.

I believe that because you picked up this book, you will be a leader who puts others first. You will be the leader who casts light on others and not darkness. You will be the leader who has earned trust and respect. You will be the leader who is slow to speak and quick to listen. You will be the leader who will stand for truth and speak for the voiceless. You will be the leader who will leave an expansive impact in every place they set foot in. You will be the leader who honors all men. Your belief system will be centered around the power of loving others. You will have acknowledged, accepted, and pronounced that leading is not about you. Organizations will do better because of your presence.

The time you spend on developing yourself is invaluable. No amount of money can match the wealth of joy, kindness, gentleness, meekness, patience, and love you will get in return.

ABOUT THE
AUTHOR

Reneé J. Murdock is the founder and CEO of 4Mosaic LLC. She is an experienced governance professional, certified trainer in leadership development, executive coaching, and neurolinguistics programming. With over fifteen years in leadership roles, she emphasizes teaching individuals to lead rather than just manage. Reneé has authored Standard Operating Procedures for various organizations, earning recognition for her loyalty and vision. Her educational background includes a Doctorate in Strategic Leadership, a Master of Science in Performance Improvement, a Bachelor of Arts in Business Leadership, and an Associate's degree in Business Administration. She has numerous certifications in leadership management, leadership development, small group facilitation, system approaches to training, instructor training, and experiential adolescent training. Reneé is a student at heart and continues ongoing education.

In addition to her extensive professional and educational background, Reneé Murdock is an avid advocate for education and personal growth. She believes in the power of leadership to inspire positive change and is committed to fostering environments where leaders not only excel but also empower those around them. Through her work as a consultant and coach, Reneé has gained a reputation for her dedication, insight, and ability to align organizational goals with practical, results-oriented strategies.

Outside of her professional pursuits, Reneé enjoys spending time with her family and participating in community service projects. Her most accomplished training experience was having her daughter, at age ten, show her the list of colleges she wanted to attend and why.

She values lifelong learning and encourages others to embrace challenges as opportunities for growth and development. Connect with Reneé through Instagram (josierc_doc), LinkedIn, and Twitter (reneemur_doc). Visit www.4mosaic.com for more information on coaching and consulting services.

www.ingramcontent.com/pod-product-compliance
Lightning Source LLC
Chambersburg PA
CBHW061140120626
46546CB00005B/1873